COLLINS COUNTRYSIDE SERIES

FOSSILS

These books are intended to offer the beginner a modern
introduction to British natural history. Written by experienced field workers who are also successful teachers, they
assume no previous training and are carefully illustrated.
It is hoped that they will help to spread understanding and
love of our wild plant and animal life, and the desire to
conserve it for the future.

COLLINS COUNTRYSIDE SERIES

FOSSILS

*

David Dineley

COLLINS
ST JAMES'S PLACE, LONDON

William Collins Sons & Co Ltd
London · Glasgow · Sydney · Auckland
Toronto · Johannesburg

First published 1979
© D. L. Dineley 1979

ISBN 0 00 219673 5

Made and printed in Great Britain by
William Collins Sons & Co Ltd Glasgow

CONTENTS

PHOTOGRAPHS

All photographs by Robin Godwin unless otherwise acknowledged

ACKNOWLEDGMENTS

IT is a pleasure to thank the good people who have been so kind and patient during the preparation of this volume in the Countryside Series. My colleagues, Dr John Cowie and Dr Keith Allen, have as ever been willing to check facts, discuss ideas and criticize the text for me. Mrs Joyce Rowland has with speed and uncanny accuracy turned my tattered manuscript into typescript without blemish, and Mrs Alma Gregory has drawn the figures with her customary skill and care. Robin Godwin has, except for a few instances acknowledged elsewhere, taken the portraits of the fossils with his usual photographic skill. The errors and blemishes that remain, despite this splendid help and the therapy that the Collins staff have effected throughout, must be attributed solely to me.

David Dineley

PREFACE

THERE are so many splendidly fossiliferous rocks in the British Isles that it is small wonder that the science of fossils – palaeontology – has flourished here. The word 'fossil' is derived from the Latin *'fossus'* (having been dug up) and in early usage it was applied to minerals and rocks as well as to the preserved remains of animals or plants. Today it is only applied to the later categories, remains of once-living things. ('Subfossils' are such objects generally less than 25,000 years old.)

From simple beginnings millions of years ago to the immense variety of living things today there has been an unbroken process of change. We call it evolution. More young people in schools, universities and elsewhere are learning about fossils than ever before, learning not only about the evolution of life on earth but also about how fossils can contribute to our understanding of the history of the planet itself. The progress of life through the ages has been very much affected by geological events and, conversely, a visitor from space would find a very different geology had there never been life on earth. In the pages that follow the reader will, I hope, see something of this relationship revealed. The book is not a field guide to fossils nor is it a textbook of palaeontology. It does not dwell upon the details of the way in which life on earth has become more diverse and complex from its beginnings thousands of millions of years ago down to the present. What it tries to do is to relate just a few of the facts and ideas that interest both geologists and palaeontologists today. Perhaps it may persuade the reader that the fossils he collects in the countryside (or the city) today are clues to an immense and complicated plot in which a few chemical elements are propelled on their course by the energies of the sun above and the earth below.

Most books about fossils are concerned with the remains of creatures that lived in the sea – shell fish, corals and the like, and they deal with these fossils zoological group by group. The plan in this account is in part to look at the fossils in groups that were the characteristic forms of life in the major environments – the open sea, the sea floor and so on. It may not be altogether the simplest or most comprehensive way of doing it, but I hope that it conveys something of the desire palaeontologists have to see individual kinds of fossil creatures as part of a very intricate web of life which in the past was as full of surprises and conundrums as it is today.

CHAPTER I

LIFE ON A WET PLANET

PERHAPS fossils hold a special fascination because they are the remains of things long since dead, extinct or dead for maybe hundreds of millions of years. The word 'fossil' is used these days not only to identify a part of an animal or plant that has been preserved in a deposit, but also to indicate any trace of the activity of organisms in that sediment before it became rock. *Trace fossils*, as the latter kind are called, may be footprints, trails, burrows, and even nests and feeding marks, and they can tell us a great deal about the kinds and numbers of animals that lived in many an ancient habitat.

Large though the number of different living things in the world is today, the total number of different kinds to have existed throughout the geological past is truly enormous. Even a brief and general acquaintance with fossils brings to one's attention the great range of sizes, shapes and anatomy that life has presented in the past. The incredibly large number of different types of fossils now recognized throughout the world is, however, thought to be only a small fraction of the total that has existed. We shall never know what the exact number has been.

A world where there had never been life would in some ways resemble the moon, but earth differs from its satellite in two ways which make it possible for life to exist here. It has the covering of gases we call the atmosphere and it is wet. Water has made possible the chemical reactions necessary for living matter to exist and reproduce itself. Somehow, back in the distant geological past, life appeared on earth and as the years have passed our planet and the living things upon it have changed. This ceaseless process of change we call evolution. For the most part it seems a slow business. Understanding the evolution of the earth from earliest times to the present is the goal of the geologist. His branch of science involves the study of rocks and the ways in which they are formed and destroyed: the palaeontologist seeks to understand the evolution of life from the evidence of *fossils*.

Fossils, then, are traces of ancient life; the buried shells, bones or petrified parts of organisms of the past or the traces of their activities are all fossils, and they can be woven into a remarkable story of evolution. We believe that today there is a close relationship between living things and the

11

place where they live – their environment. If it were the same in the past, as seems likely, then the palaeontologist needs the help of the geologist to tell him what the earth was like then. In fact these two kinds of scientist need each other's assistance very often.

In this book we are going to look at how the flimsy and fleeting forms of life that have passed across the face of the earth have left a record in the seemingly permanent rocks which occur over so much of our continents. Discoveries of fossils help scientists answer questions about the living world but they also prompt other questions which are by no means near to being answered yet. Some of these conundrums will become apparent as we proceed.

Geologists have used a very convenient rule of thumb when trying to unravel geological history, namely that the present is the key to the past. They can for the most part explain earth history in terms of the kinds of geological processes going on today. Volcanic eruptions, floods and the destruction of the coastline by the sea are examples of different geological processes which from time to time are obvious to us all, but there are many others quietly and imperceptibly changing the landscape. Even when the earth was much younger these processes may have been as effective and widespread as they are now. And in very many of them there was a common and essential agent – water.

WATER EVERYWHERE

When the earth was newly formed from a mass of dust and gases in the primeval solar nebula it may have looked rather like our cratered and pock-marked moon today. Such atmosphere as there was was rich in hydrogen and as the sun's energy intensified so that as its radiation, the solar wind, grew strong this atmosphere was blown away. Some tens of millions of years later the earth itself grew hot and molten and volcanic activity broke out everywhere. Gases which had been long-trapped in the interior of the planet began to find their way to the surface. At the surface these gases were too heavy to be blown away by the solar wind and they began to accumulate as an atmosphere of carbon dioxide, methane, ammonia, sulphurous gases and water. The water condensed as the earth's surface gradually cooled, and the oceans came into being. As rain, rivers, lakes and oceans spread over the surface so chemical reactions took place and the processes of erosion by water and by wind began their task. Liquid water has remained as the principal means by which eroded material has been carried from the mountains out to the continental shelves and even into the ocean deeps.

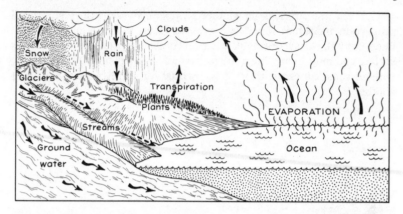

Water is one of the most important features on the surface of the earth in that it is essential for so many geological processes and for the existence of life. There is a constant movement of water between the oceans, the atmosphere and the land.

In those early days, as at present, there was a complex relationship between the waters of the earth (the hydrosphere) and the gases above them, the atmosphere. Weather (and climate) would have depended very largely upon this, as it still does. Chemical processes of rock destruction and formation would have been influenced by the water and atmosphere, and eventually life itself was evolved in the shelter of earth's envelope of atmosphere and hydrosphere. As time went on, the accumulation of gas and water reached a level not very different from that of today though its composition may have been different. Little oxygen in the air and little salt in the sea may have been the general state then. From an atmosphere rich in carbon dioxide to one rich in oxygen the change has been made by two thousand million years of the activity of the photosynthetic plants. The oceans rapidly became salt from a chain of reactions between atmosphere, hydrosphere and the volcanic rocks that seem always to have been associated with the oceanic hollows on the surface of the earth. Sea water seems to have been of the same composition for most of its subsequent history.

That water moves from place to place in the air as clouds, in rivers and as currents in the sea is plain enough. The heat of the sun keeps it moving, though sometimes to our discomfort the rate is rather variable. A simplified version of the way in which water moves is shown in our diagram of the hydrological cycle and in some form or other a hydrological cycle must have existed for as long as there has been water.

Today over 97 per cent of all water is contained in the world's oceans;

glaciers and ice-caps lock up another 2.15 per cent while the rest, a small proportion indeed, is found in rivers, in lakes, in the atmosphere and underground. Not surprisingly, water covers about 71 per cent of the earth's surface and most living things are found in it. Few organisms can live long without some contact with it; it is essential for all life – in one form or another.

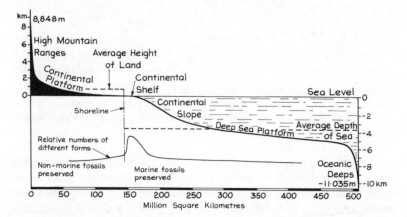

The hypsometric curve shows the way in which the areas of the earth's surface from highest mountain to ocean deep are distributed. Most forms of life are to be found between 2 km above and 2 km below sea level and it is in this region that the greatest variety of sedimentary rocks with fossils originates. The inset graph shows that most of the commonly preserved fossils belong to the shallow marine realm, the continental shelf. (After Holmes).

So for the vast majority of living things water is an essential part of the place in which they live, their habitat, and wherever water exists life is found, even in the snows of the highest mountains, the hot pools of volcanic areas and the ice of Antarctica. In the seas and oceans of the world waters may be very salty or be very deep and cold. Life has adapted to meet these conditions, but it is most prolific and varied in the shallow, warm, clear and sunny waters around the continents and islands of the world. Indeed depth, temperature, oxygen and salinity are the most important factors regulating the distribution of life in the seas. It appears always to have been so. Life is crowded in narrow realms of favourable conditions; as these conditions fade or depart so the spread of living things becomes thinner and more space is needed to support fewer organisms.

Thus water has played a vital part in controlling where life has spread during much of its history. As seas have advanced over and retreated from the continents, life has accompanied them and evolved to fill the new environments created. As seas have deposited their layers of sediment, life has left its traces ranging from microscopic shells to hundreds of square miles of coral reefs. Sediments and organisms have become rocks and fossils in a bewildering array of kinds and with an ever-changing pattern in time and space.

SEDIMENTARY ROCKS

No book about fossils should omit a word or two on sedimentary rocks, for most fossils occur in those formations. Sedimentary rocks are familiar features of the landscape in most countries and we can almost see everywhere some of the processes going on which lead to the formation of these, the stratified or bedded rocks. As the name suggests, sedimentary rocks owe their origin to the accumulation of sediment which may have been mud, sand, peat or soil or perhaps desert or volcanic dust. In the course of time the originally loose or sloppy sediment may become compacted, hardened and cemented into a cohesive mass, layer upon layer. Very often the geologist can from the study of such a rock suggest the conditions under which the original sediment accumulated. Some of his evidence may be the fossils that the rock contains: and from a study of the rock he may also be able to say something about the habitat and history of the organisms that became the fossils.

All the rocks at the surface of the earth are at the mercy of the atmosphere, water, heat and cold and living things. Chemical decay and organic attack aid the enormous work of rock weathering carried out by purely physical agencies such as the sun's heat and winter's frosts. Rock weathering produces sediment – clay and sand – and minerals in solution, all of which are slowly removed by streams and, sometimes, the wind. Most sediment eventually reaches the sea where it is spread over the sea floor by tides, currents and storms as a destinct layer, and this may in time form a *detrital* or *clastic* rock, one formed of (rock and mineral) particles derived from elsewhere. In many cases the particles are pieces of shell or some other hard material once part of a living sea creature.

The process of turning sands and other loose materials into rock is called lithification. It can be a complex affair but basically it involves the cementing of the grains together and the general squeezing and compacting of the material under its own weight and that of later deposits on top.

Some rocks consist almost entirely of what we normally regard as

soluble materials, as distinct from relatively insoluble grains and fragments. These *chemical* rocks include salt deposits, limestones and dolo-
mites. There are also a few chemical rocks which consist of silica, phosphate,
ironstone and other materials.

Sedimentary rocks may have other distinguishing characteristics which
separate them from the volcanic or other crystalline formations. They
commonly show bedding planes, the more or less parallel partings which
separate successive rock layers or strata from one another. Many bedding
planes are smooth and flat, others may be highly irregular. Bedding planes
may also bear distinctive features such as footprints, rain spots, ripple-
marks, and scour-marks left on the sediment layer before it was buried and
hardened. They may also be crowded with fossils.

Between bedding planes there may be other features which bear witness
to the origin of the rock. The layers themselves may have been disturbed
by subsequent movement and while the sediment was still unconsolidated,
the burrowing activities of worms, molluscs and other creatures would
tend to disrupt and change its original layering.

Thus these rock formations contain clues of many kinds relating to the
world of the past, its climates, topography and inhabitants. Many of them
are formed from the shells or other hard parts of different organisms in
countless millions. They provide the background against which to see
fossils and from which a long and very eventful story may be construed.

THE GEOLOGICAL CYCLE

The map of the world shows us a seemingly uneven distribution of land
and ocean, with great mountain chains, plainlands, shallow seas and very
deep wide oceans. Rivers drain the land and, with their mud and sand,
pour into the sea along almost every coastline. Elsewhere volcanoes are
active, building up cones and ridges of new volcanic rock, lava, ash and
dust. New rock is attacked by the atmosphere until in time it breaks down
into a soil or sediment. In turn this is washed, rolled or blown into the
rivers, ultimately to be borne out to the sea. Layer upon layer of sand and
mud so accumulating over the years is compacted and compressed under
its growing weight so that the layers become hardened into layers of
sedimentary rock.

With the continuous movement of the earth's crust, masses of sedimentary and other rocks are carried deep into the earth where they are
transformed by the great heat and pressure into molten material once
again. The matter once present in a new volcanic lava can thus be changed
into a sediment, made into a sedimentary rock, and then perhaps returned

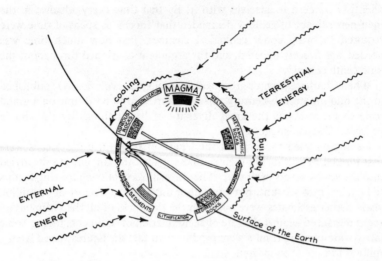

The geological cycle is the pattern of movement and the transformations that affect rocks in the crust of the earth. While new rocks are constantly being formed others are suffering destruction. In terms of human or animal life spans the cycle is very slow-moving indeed.

to something like its original form. This sequence of events has been called the *geological cycle*. It is a slow-moving cycle compared with the pace of events in, say, human history, and it has been kept moving by the energy of the sun's rays, the weather and the heat within the earth itself.

No matter how slow the geological cycle seems to be, it has made enormous changes to the surface of our planet, and it shows no signs of coming to a halt. It has been constantly changing the geological background to the evolution of life and thus, we might reasonably believe, influencing the course of life itself.

GEOLOGICAL TIME

In the normal course of history we measure time by the passing of years – the time it takes for the earth to orbit once round the sun. For geological purposes a year is so small a unit as to be insignificant; we need to think in terms of *millions* of years, and that is a very difficult thing to do.

It was natural for historians in early times to ask how far back history went and for early man himself to have mystical or religious ideas about the origin of the world. Only towards the end of the eighteenth century did scientists concern themselves with it. By that time every advance in the then-new science of geology demanded that enormous spans of time were required to bring about geological changes. Just how much time was needed was fiercely debated, and the argument continued throughout the nineteenth century.

When Charles Darwin's great work on biological evolution was published in the mid nineteenth-century this, too, appeared to need time on a grand scale to bring about the great diversity of living things by the simple processes Darwin suggested.

Geologists tried to work out the length of time since the oceans were first formed by measuring their saltiness against the amount of salt carried into the sea by rivers each year. There are all sorts of complicating factors to be taken into account, but one author did arrive at a figure of 90 million years. Other estimates were based on the thickness of all the sedimentary rocks measured against the rate of accumulation of sediments today. Some fairly wide-ranging results were produced, in fact the figures varied from 3 million to over 1500 million.

Physicists took an interest in the problem and began to think of age in terms of heat loss from the earth and the sun but by the end of last century they did not suggest anything more than 100 million years. Then after the

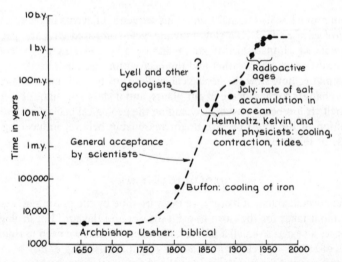

Changes in ideas about the magnitude of geological time are shown in this graph. The increasing pace of science generally is also reflected in the curve. (After Press and Siever).

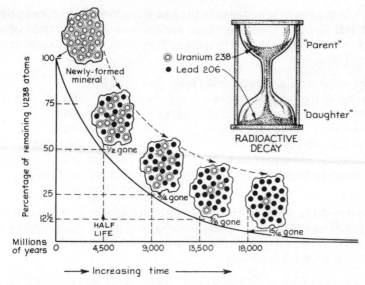

The measurement of geological time has been perhaps most effectively made by studies of radioactivity. Radioactive elements break down as is shown in the case above of uranium 238 changing to lead 206. The arrowed line traces the slow disintegration of uranium over thousands of millions of years. The means of measuring these changes involve very accurate measurement of tiny quantities of elements, a delicate and costly business.

discovery of radioactivity a new approach became possible. It was realized that radioactive elements change into other elements; uranium, for example, slowly produced helium and lead. Lord Rutherford, one of the foremost physicists at the University of Cambridge, in 1906 made the first attempt to find the age of radioactive minerals from the ratio of uranium and helium present in them. The principle was soon taken up and the analytical processes were developed and refined by other scientists. It has been used ever since and several different kinds of analysis are now possible. They all reveal the proportions of 'parent' and 'daughter' elements in a mineral, and knowing the rate at which the transformation of the one to the other takes place we can compute how long it has been since the mineral was formed. Radioactivity has provided us with a geological clock at least for those rocks in which some radioactive minerals are present.

All of which is very well, but it does not help most of us to grasp the magnitude of geological time – the four and a half thousand million years of it which seems to be indicated by the geological clock. To give some help with this several schemes have been devised. One such is to think of a single year as representing the 4500 million years since the earth first formed: then –

the oldest remaining rocks dated from	– mid March
primitive forms of life appeared	– May
the first land plants and animals evolved	– late November
the Coal age forests flourished	– early December
the dinosaur heyday	– about 15 December
the first appearance of man	– late evening 31 December
Columbus discovered America	– 3 seconds to midnight, 31 December

So it might be said that the vast majority of fossils were produced only in the last quarter of this 'year'. Many of the great events in organic evolution were 'autumnal'. Like Cinderella, we may wonder what will happen once midnight has finished striking.

THE GEOLOGICAL RECORD

While the men in the laboratories have been working to provide a geological clock the geologists in the field have been piecing together the events that have taken up so much of geological time. It is a story of great changes, and in it the crust of the earth appears to be much more mobile than was thought only twenty years ago. We have known for a long time that rock formations produced under icy conditions at one period of earth history lie alongside or above those formed in hot environments. Changes in climate seem to have been common and perhaps extreme. Then there is the strange distribution of certain rocks and fossils which seems to imply that areas now widely separated were once close together. Moreover, from time to time the record was, it appears, upset by sudden and violent upheavals, crumpling and altering the existing rock formations. To explain it on a world-wide basis is difficult but not impossible. First let us look at the general run of events from the evidence of the oldest rocks and their successors: then later we can see how it may be accounted for and what its significance is for fossils.

Several lines of evidence suggest that the earth was formed as a planet about 4500 million years ago but not until 800 or so million years later was its surface cooled and formed into land and ocean areas. Such continents as there were may have been small and there was very great volcanic activity. By about 2900 to 2500 million years ago the crust had given rise to

YEARS BEFORE PRESENT	LITHOSPHERE	BIOSPHERE	HYDROSPHERE	ATMOSPHERE
20 MILLION	GLACIATION	MAMMALS DIVERSIFY GRASSES APPEAR		OXYGEN APPROACHES PRESENT LEVEL
50 MILLION	COAL FORMATION VOLCANISM			
100 MILLION		SOCIAL INSECTS, FLOWERING PLANTS MAMMALS		ATMOSPHERIC OXYGEN INCREASES AT FLUCTUATING RATE
200 MILLION	GREAT VOLCANISM COAL FORMATION	INSECTS APPEAR LAND PLANTS APPEAR	OCEANS CONTINUE TO INCREASE IN VOLUME	
500 MILLION	GLACIATION (An "ice age")	METAZOA APPEAR RAPID INCREASE IN PHYTOPLANKTON	SURFACE WATERS OPENED TO PHYTOPLANKTON	OXYGEN AT 3-10 PERCENT OF PRESENT ATMOSPHERIC LEVEL
1 THOUSAND MILLION	VOLCANISM (= Volcanic eruptions on a grand scale)	EUCARYOTES		OXYGEN AT 1 PERCENT OF PRESENT ATMOSPHERIC LEVEL, OZONE SCREEN EFFECTIVE
2 THOUSAND MILLION	GLACIATION	ADVANCED OXYGEN-MEDIATING ENZYMES	OXYGEN DIFFUSES INTO ATMOSPHERE	OXYGEN INCREASING, CARBON DIOXIDE DECREASING OXYGEN IN ATMOSPHERE
5 THOUSAND MILLION	OLDEST SEDIMENTS OLDEST EARTH ROCKS (ORIGIN OF SOLAR SYSTEM)	FIRST OXYGEN-GENERATING PHOTOSYNTHETIC CELLS PROCARYOTES ABIOGENIC EVOLUTION ("pre-organic" and chemical evolution)	ORIGIN OF OCEANS	NO FREE OXYGEN

The geological record is shown in outline here. Important events in the history of the solid earth, of the waters, atmosphere, and of the life upon it are indicated. The length of time during which fossils have been found is relatively very small compared with the full span of earth's existence.

continents not much different in total area from those of today. The geological cycle had by then been active long enough to produce many different kinds of landscapes but the atmosphere was at that time probably made much more of carbon dioxide than of oxygen. Life had begun in the waters of the earth and the oldest fossils were already formed.

As time progressed the continents changed their shapes and positions on the earth's surface. The landscapes were largely if not entirely devoid of vegetation and the rains ran unhindered into the water courses. Volcanic activity at sea and on land broke out locally and was indeed probably going on unceasingly in the oceanic areas.

On at least two occasions within the last 1000 million years the continents seem to have been grouped together in a single great cluster. When this occurred some areas became arid deserts while others seem to have been covered in ice, like Antarctica today. Such changes would have very important consequences for the living things of those days.

One of the effects of locking up great volumes of water in the form of huge ice-caps may have been the effective lowering of sea level. The sea would thus be withdrawn from those shallow areas about the land masses which we know as the continental shelves. These are very important areas because they support many kinds of life and they are where many of the sediments of the past – our present sedimentary rocks – have formed.

There were several periods in earth-history when the seas do seem to have retreated from the lands and others when the seas spread out far and wide across the continents. Changes of these kinds too would affect the living world of that day.

Our knowledge of this kind of change over the last 600 million years or so is much better than of previous events, largely because until then there were very few fossils being produced. Life was largely confined to small soft-bodied organisms, lacking hard parts. Study of the fossils which began then to appear in the record has helped solve many of the problems about the geography of those past times.

The figure on p. 21 shows some of the major changes and events that we think have taken place over this last 600 million years.

A RELATIVE TIME-SCALE

Long before a means of finding the ages of the rocks in rather large and approximate numbers of years had been discovered, geologists had drawn up a time-scale in which the time periods were defined as those during which certain groups of strata had been laid down. Some of these rock units are very thick, others are thin but their value lies in the facts that each is characterized by distinctive fossils and that from one place to another these rocks can be seen resting one upon another in a recognizable order. Unless something very peculiar has happened the oldest rocks underlie the others and those at the top of the pile are the youngest of all. By observing the order of succession, as it is called, and recording the kinds of fossils present in each layer, a simple table could be drawn up. The table of names given to these rocks and to the periods of time during which they were formed has evolved over the years. As most of this pioneering work was done in western Europe, most of the names are associated with this region.

It was very soon realized that between some adjacent groups of rocks there are big differences and that their fossils too show many dissimilarities.

At one time it was believed that these changes were brought about by universal catastrophies with the extinction of all forms of life. After each such catastrophe, creation produced new and more complicated organisms afresh. However, in other parts of the world now known to us it is obvious that no such catastrophies occurred and that no great break in the stream of life occurred. Nevertheless, for large periods of time and for groups of rocks separated in Europe by such breaks, we retain the names *Palaeozoic* (ancient life), *Mesozoic* (middle life), *Cainozoic* (recent life). Two other names have been coined as well – *Cryptozoic* (hidden life) for the Precambrian times

ERA	SYSTEM OR PERIOD	EPOCH
CENOZOIC (*recent life*)	QUATERNARY (an addition to the old tripartite 18th-century classification)	RECENT PLEISTOCENE (*most recent*) PLIOCENE (*very recent*) MIOCENE (*moderately recent*)
	TERTIARY (Third, from the 18th-century classification)	OLIGOCENE (*slightly recent*) EOCENE (*dawn of the recent*) PALAEOCENE (*early dawn of the recent*)
MESOZOIC (*middle life*)	CRETACEOUS (from the Latin for chalk)	
	JURASSIC (Jura Mountains, Europe)	
	TRIASSIC (from tripartite division in Germany)	
PALAEOZOIC (*ancient life*)	PERMIAN (Perm, a province of Russia)	
	CARBONIFEROUS (from abundant coal in rocks) PENNSYLVANIAN ⎺⎺ Terms used in U.S.A., MISSISSIPPIAN ⎺⎺ equivalent to Carboniferous	
	DEVONIAN (Devonshire, England)	
	SILURIAN (the Silures, an ancient British tribe)	
	ORDOVICIAN (the Ordovices, an ancient British tribe)	
	CAMBRIAN (Roman name for Wales)	
PRECAMBRIAN	Many local systems and series are recognised, but no well-established world-wide classification has yet been attained.	

The stratigraphic column is the geologist's version of the order in which geological formations have been laid down; these *systems* of rock have given their names to *periods* of geological time covering the last 600 million years.

and rocks and *Phanerozoic* (apparent life) for the rocks of Cambrian and later dates.

The different geological periods shown in the figure on p. 23 are named either after places where their representative rocks occur or after a physical attribute. There has not always been agreement amongst geologists as to how this should be done and some famous squabbles have broken out on this score as the science of geology has progressed. At the base of our Phanerozoic column we have the CAMBRIAN system. It takes its name from the ancient name for Wales where it was studied by Adam Sedgwick, the first professor of geology at the University of Cambridge early in the nineteenth century. The ORDOVICIAN system was only so named as late as 1879 by Charles Lapworth. The Ordovices were a Celtic tribe inhabiting parts of Wales and the Welsh Borderland during Roman times. Lapworth coined the name for rocks which included some that Sedgwick had called Cambrian and others which had been included in the SILURIAN system by another eminent nineteenth-century geologist, Sir Roderick Murchison. As it happened, Sedgwick and Murchison had begun to work together in Wales, Sedgwick studying the rocks at the bottom of the fossiliferous sequence and working upwards while from the base of the Old Red Sandstone Murchison worked down through the sequence. Eventually a sharp dispute arose between these two friends as to the common boundary between their rock systems. Alas, the controversy continued for about thirty years and was only settled when Lapworth produced what might be described as a characteristic British compromise. Only gradually did American and European geologists take up this arrangement but it now seems to be universally recognized. The Silurian system, too, was named after a Celtic tribe, the Silures, who inhabited the Welsh Borderland area of Britain some 2000 years ago.

The DEVONIAN system was named after that county by Sedgwick and Murchison in 1840, in the happy days before their estrangement. Its fossils seemed at first to be akin either to those of the CARBONIFEROUS rocks or to those of the Silurian. In fact closer examination showed them to be distinct from those of either of the other systems and the Devonian strata were found clearly occupying a place equivalent to the Old Red Sandstone of South Wales, that is between the Silurian and the Carboniferous. The coal-bearing nature of the Carboniferous rocks prompted William Coneybeare to suggest the name in 1822. North American geologists have tended to use the names Mississippian and Pennsylvanian for two systems in place of the single Carboniferous system.

The PERMIAN system is another one coined by Murchison (in 1841), and it is based on the rocks he saw in the Russian province of Perm while

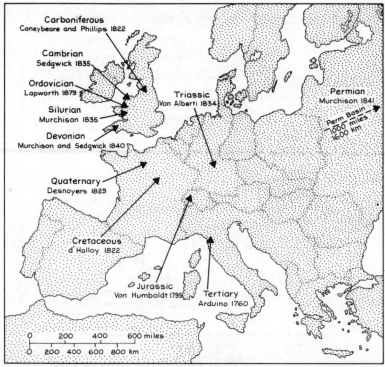

The type areas of various geological systems are the places where those
rocks were first scientifically described. Most of the names in common use
are of places in western Europe, (but see fig. on p. 23).

carrying out a geological reconnaissance for the Czar. Lying upon the
Permian strata are those of the TRIASSIC system, a division named by
Friedrich von Alberti in 1834 because of the three series of rocks that seem
so inseparable over much of Germany. Together these two systems are
often called the New Red Sandstone.

JURASSIC rocks crop out in splendid array in the Jura Mountains of
France and were first so designated by the German scientist Alexander von
Humboldt in 1795. They are also very fossiliferous, which attracted
attention to them. However, the Jurassic system of rocks as a distinct group
in its own right was first recognized by a German geologist and palaeontologist, Leopold von Buch, in 1839.

The Latin word for chalk is *creta* and the CRETACEOUS system certainly
has its share of that peculiar limestone. The title was proposed by the

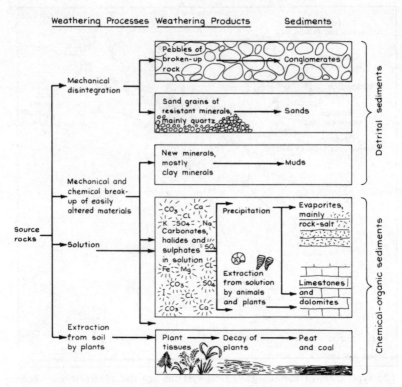

A broad classification of the two main kinds of sedimentary rocks. (After Read and Watson).

Belgian geologist Omalius d'Halloy in 1822 for the chalk and associated beds of the Paris area. Today considerably more than the chalky strata is included within this system.

The TERTIARY systems were defined by Charles Lyell in 1833 in what was then a new way – by the relative proportions of the living and extinct species each contained. For example the Eocene contained 3 per cent of living species, the Miocene 17 per cent, the Pliocene 50 to 67 per cent. In 1839 he followed with the Pleistocene for the deposits of the glacial ages which precede the Recent (postglacial) deposits. The Ogligocene and Palaeocene series were later additions to the scale by other geologists.

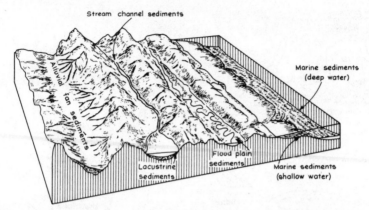

Areas where sedimentary rock may form from sediments. Most sediment is ultimately deposited in the sea where it largely comes to rest in relatively shallow water. On the land sediment may be deposited in river valleys and flood plains, in lakes and in coastal swamps. (After Fagan).

THE LIVING DEAD

How, in fact, do palaeontologists distinguish one kind of fossil from another? For the most part they have adopted the simple practice of comparing fossils with present-day organisms and then giving names to the fossils that suggest the possible relationships they have with modern forms. Of course this works satisfactorily where the fossils are well preserved, numerous and rather like familiar animals or plants. Where the fossil is quite unlike anything known alive today the problem is more difficult. Most fossils to which names have been given so far seem to be akin to things alive today, but the known number of curious forms which seem to bear no relationship at all to life about us now increases each year.

Zoologists and botanists need a method of naming their specimens that everyone will accept and use – a common language for identifying individuals and groups of organisms. The system in use almost everywhere today was invented about two hundred years ago by a remarkable Swedish naturalist, Carl Linnéus. He produced a simple but effective scheme by arranging the known animals and plants into groups on the basis of their similarities. Groups in turn were placed into larger categories and these in still larger units, each having a number of characteristics shared by all its members. Not only is the arrangement visually useful but it is also a way of attempting to recognize and record the 'family tree' relationships of

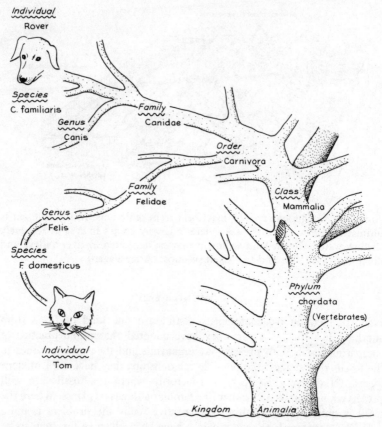

The Linnéan system of names applied to household animals, the dog, *Canis familiaris* and the cat *Felis domesticus*. Fossils are treated in the same way as far as possible.

different living things. For example, our household pets *Canis familiaris* and *Felis domesticus* are the Linnéan names for two species of mammals which belong to different families but to the same order. Naturally there has been a bit of squabbling about the names to be given to newly found creatures when their discoverers have published descriptions and (new) names for them. On the whole, however, Linnéus's system has worked well since it was invented and has not needed to be refined very much. Very many kinds of plants, creatures and fossils have been added to the list since

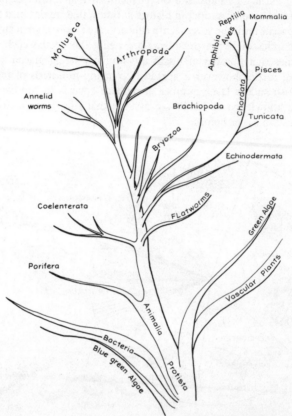

A suggested family tree for some major groups of living organisms.

Linnéus's day and other schemes have been devised to accommodate some of the less easily understood kinds of fossils.

As we might expect, most fossils are indeed named on the Linnéan plan, but many palaeontologists have different ideas on precisely how it should be done. Recognizing a 'new' species from fragmentary fossil evidence may be a very uncertain and difficult business and the temperaments of some scientists have led them into fierce conflict with their fellows over which of them has described or named certain species correctly or best.

It seems that there are about one and a half million species of known organisms in the world today. Most of them are well established and successful, as far as we can see, but others are close to dying out – to becoming extinct perhaps as a direct result of man's interference. Some animals have become extinct in historical times, that quaint bird that lived in Madagascar until the seventeenth century, the Dodo, is such an example.

New species of living organisms are being discovered each year and many times that number of fossils are similarly being placed on record. The fossil record however is spread over many hundreds of millions of years. With such a large number of modern species to contemplate and with our knowledge of fossils we assume that life is more diverse and successful than ever before.

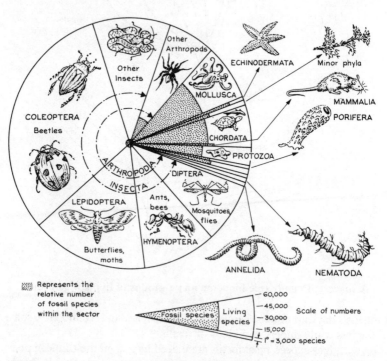

Numbers of fossil and living organisms. The number of previously unknown living animals and plants is rising today relatively slowly. New species of fossil animals and plants are being described in great numbers each year. (After Miller and Campbell).

A question that arises at this stage naturally enough is to what extent the fossil record may be relied upon as a true guide to the variety and abundance of life in bygone ages. It is largely a matter of the 'preservability' of traces of animals and plants in the environments in which they live and die. About one-sixth of all modern species of animals live in the sea and perhaps half of these live on the sandy or muddy sea floor. Maybe about half of the dwellers on the sea bed possess some hard parts or skeleton which may remain after the animal dies. Buried in sediment, these hard items may in time become fossils. On the face of it, less than 15 per cent of all living marine species are likely to become fossils. There seems to be no reason to believe that the proportion was higher in the past: the modern sample is probably comparable with those of ancient sea faunas.

Although the number is increasing each year, we know rather less than 150,000 species of such fossils as yet. (The proportion of fossil plants known is even smaller.) These are mostly of creatures that have hard parts of calcium phosphate, calcium carbonate, silica or chitin – teeth, bones, and the like. To find any trace of soft tissues is very rare.

The numbers of modern species most susceptible to fossilization in having some hard preservable tissues are:-

Invertebrates	170,000
Vertebrates	49,000
Vascular plants	350,000
A total of	569,000 species

Some very simple plant species (algae for example) may be preserved because they secrete amounts of durable calcium carbonate.

The number of individuals in a species can be very great, protozoa, flies or midges for example, and in spite of all the hazards that make fossilization so rare an event, fossils are not really uncommon. In many fossil species the numbers of individuals are fantastically abundant.

How many fossil species have there been? It is the kind of question to which an answer is rather meaningless; the figure is of astronomical size. Evidence from many quarters suggests that individual fossil species lasted on average up to twelve million years, and the number of plant and animal species that may be preserved in the rocks could be more than ten million. Countless other species have passed away leaving no trace of their existence. Getting to know something about those species that are abundantly preserved is a major task: we can only wonder about the remainder.

Not all life has lived in the sea, and the ancient floras and faunas on the land and in the rivers and lakes were no doubt subject to the same hazards that prevent their fossilization as are modern animals and plants in these environments.

Although many creatures in the sea bequeath their remains to the sea floor sediments round about, land animals are rarely preserved as fossils unless their remains fall into accumulating sediments such as lakes, bogs or, of course, the sea. They are removed from where they lived to a natural site of burial. This is one of the reasons why fossil birds are so rare and fossil shellfish so common, relatively speaking. The fossil record is thus not a random sample of past life but is rather a selected sample of organisms that lived in or near a place where sediments were accumulating. It is a record dependent upon geological events as well as biological factors.

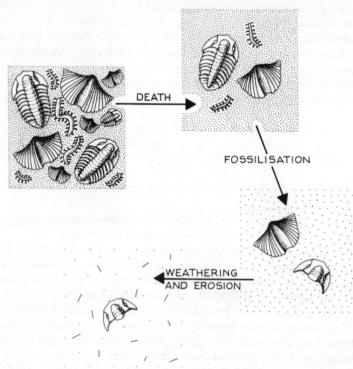

DEATH

FOSSILISATION

WEATHERING AND EROSION

Fossils in the rock most commonly are only a very small number of those organisms that were originally present in the living fauna of the day. Mortality removes a large part of the fauna from a 'sample'. Preservation of those remains by fossilization may also be selective and so reduce the numbers further and many more specimens may be destroyed by later changes in the rock or at the surface of the ground before the collector can pick up a lone fragment from a once-numerous community. (After Beerbower).

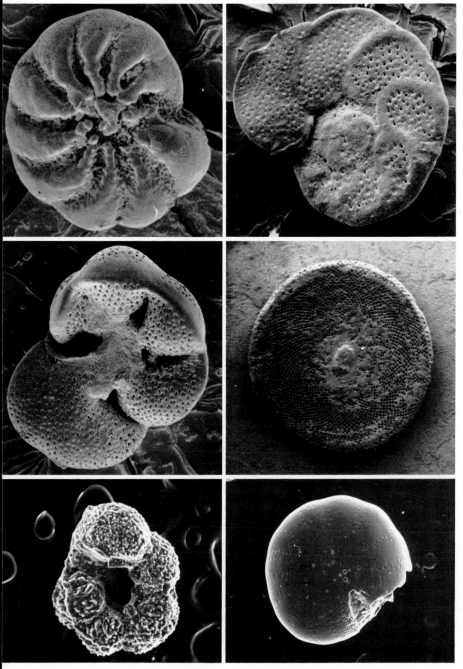

PLATE I. Common microfossils in rocks of marine origin are foraminifera. Typical forms from Mesozoic and Cainozoic formations are *top
left, Nonion* (× 35), *right, Cibicides* (× 35); *centre left, Discorbis* (× 35),
right, Orbitolites (× 30), all from the Eocene; *bottom left, Globotruncana*
(× 40), Cretaceous, *right, Elphidiella* (× 30), Pleistocene.

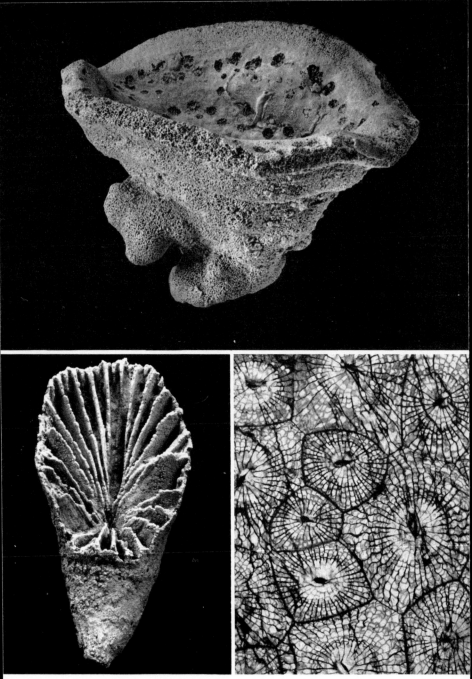

PLATE 2. *Above*, the small Cretaceous sponge, *Rhaphidonema* (× 1)
showing its spongy structure; *below left, Zaphrentis* (× 2) a small 'horn
coral' from the Carboniferous Limestone; *right*, a cross-section of a colony
of the rugose coral *Lithostrotion* (× 1) shows typical septa and other
structures of calcium carbonate.

In recent years palaeontologists have been taking a further look at the numbers of different species of shallow sea-dwelling fossil creatures that there have been since the beginning of the Cambrian period. One estimate is that the number of marine invertebrate species with preservable hard parts to be found as fossils has increased from around 100,000 to over 1,000,000 since mid-Palaeozoic time. That is a very large increase indeed and the estimate has been criticized quite severely. Nevertheless, while there is no denying that the numbers of species in question are very significantly different, there does seem to be evidence that the fossil record is affected by a number of things which tend to decrease the apparent numbers of different species in older rocks. One such factor may be simply the amounts of sedimentary rocks we have available for study from each geological age. The younger rocks tend to cover the older ones so we can search for fossils from the former over the wider areas.

Another idea that has been put forward recently is that there is after all no really compelling evidence that in the shallow marine realm a worldwide long-term trend towards increased diversity of invertebrate species has existed since Cambrian time began. At that time the shallow marine environment acquired as many different kinds of invertebrate animals as it could support. Although the actual species have changed with time there may actually be no more of them now than there was then. The sea floor, has, so to speak, been saturated with living things throughout all that long time. Many palaeontologists find it hard to believe that the diversity of animals in any marine environment has not increased with time; they think that where large numbers of individuals of few species may have lived in the past rather smaller numbers of more numerous species live today. The ceaseless competition between living species for space, food and shelter – and the evolution it has set in motion – has produced some very complex relationships between species today. It must have had simple beginnings, but identifying them from fossils is very difficult indeed, if not impossible.

FOSSILIZATION

So far we have seen that fossils resemble, to a greater or less degree, modern animals and plants. They normally occur in sedimentary rocks or, in rare cases, in volcanic rocks, and have been preserved through time by the protective layers of sediment and rock around them. Only very exceptionally are organisms preserved which are the almost unaltered remains of an animal or plant. The mammoths found in the frozen bogs of Siberia are perhaps the most striking examples. They were small hairy elephants

F.   C living in the forests of the Ice Age. Although they are now extinct, several such almost complete animals have been found preserved, so to speak, in a geological deep freeze, together with the plants that were alive with them.

Much more common and much less spectacular are the altered remains of shelly or bony creatures. The vast majority of fossils have undergone some alteration since the death of the organisms. The complex chemical materials that are built up during life break down, some rapidly, some slowly after death. The simplest kind of alteration to shells, teeth, bone and other relatively less destructible materials is to a less complex chemical composition by dissolving of soluble components.

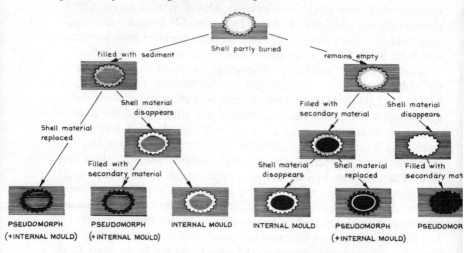

Shell partly buried

filled with sediment   remains empty

Shell material disappears   Filled with secondary material   Shell material disappears

Shell material replaced   Filled with secondary material   Shell material disappears   Shell material replaced   Filled with secondary mat

PSEUDOMORPH (+INTERNAL MOULD)   PSEUDOMORPH (+INTERNAL MOULD)   INTERNAL MOULD   INTERNAL MOULD   PSEUDOMORPH (+INTERNAL MOULD)   PSEUDOMOR

Some ways in which a shell may become fossilized.

Distillation is the kind of decomposition in which heat and pressure tend to drive out water, oxygen, hydrogen and nitrogen from the organic material. All that may remain is a black carbonaceous film, as in the case of many plant fossils. These are, in fact, thin layers of a sort of coal.

Quite commonly shells or bones have been altered or even completely replaced by minerals. This seems to be brought about by contact with percolating water in which the minerals are present. The original mineral (or plant) material is dissolved away and new mineral matter takes its place. In the process the structures of the fossil may be seriously harmed, but in some instances it is faithfully preserved even down to the smallest detail. The process of replacement is called *mineralization* or *petrifaction*. Calcite and silica (quartz) are the commonest two minerals to be present in fossils due to this process, but others such as pyrite (iron sulphide) are locally important in replacing fossil tissues. When all the original material is gone the fossil is called a *pseudomorph*.

Moulds or *impressions* are left in any soft mud or sand capable of retaining an imprint and which in time becomes a rock. The cavity left when a fossil shell falls from the rock is just such a mould or impression. Were it to be filled by a later mineral deposit a *cast* would be formed. Hollow shells may be infilled at some stage after burial, and the infilling is sometimes referred to as a *core* or *steinkern*. In most fossiliferous rock formations fossils are preserved in several different ways. As often as not, the surface weathering of the rock rather than the early mineralogical changes within the rock seems to control whether the fossils can be extracted in one form or another. Before it rests in a collector's bag a fossil may have had a very complicated chemical history. Most fossils never reach such an exalted end; for them it is just ashes to ashes and dust to dust in the rock cycle.

LIFE BEFORE FOSSILS

Searching far back into the geological past we find that most rocks older than about six hundred million years lack fossils: only in relatively very few cases can we identify older forms of life. The earliest Cambrian fossils are quite complicated and suggest highly evolved marine organisms which had unknown ancestors. Most of the Precambrian traces of life are by no means the most primitive that we can imagine. Simple plants and small animals are represented in the Precambrian fossil list of nearly every continent, while some resemble modern types. A few of the most ancient fossils are unlike anything we know today. Indeed some 'fossils' are such primitive and simple affairs that they may not be organic at all, but merely structures of mineral origin.

The instances where Precambrian organisms have become fossilized indicate unusual circumstances. For example, in the Gunflint chert of Ontario, Canada, a remarkable range of primitive plants – microscopic algae, fungi and bacteria – has been preserved in very fine silica. How this came about is uncertain, but it affords us a remarkably intimate view of a microbiological community alive about 1600 million years ago.

Our search for the earliest traces of life in the rocks, and indeed for the origin of life itself, is not confined merely to looking for fossils in the usual sense of the word. Even the simplest organisms of the present are made of protoplasm, and what versatile stuff protoplasm is. On analysis it is found to consist of very complex molecules containing primarily carbon, hydrogen, oxygen and a host of other elements in very minor quantities. Life is based on the chemistry of carbon, and when the temperatures or pressures range outside the fairly close-set limits for the necessary chemical reactions to take place, life cannot exist. For the most part, we can say that where there is water life is possible; it is a substance essential for the chemical activity of living things.

This bit of knowledge seems to narrow down the period of time and the range of conditions of rock formation in which life – and hence, fossils – could have existed. Until the earth had cooled to something like its present state it would have been difficult for life to exist. The oldest rocks show signs of the existence of water and possibly still contain clues about the earliest forms of life.

Chemists and biologists have long dreamed of discovering how to 'invent' living matter but so far have had to be content with finding out how the various biochemical materials involved in living things are made up from simpler substances. They have thus begun to trace the long chain of events leading to the formation of life from non-living material. Experiments designed to tell us something of these events have been successful in several ways. When an electric spark is caused in a mixture of water vapour, methane gas and other gases which can occur naturally in the atmosphere, some of the molecules begin to link up into more complex arrangements. They produce what are called *amino-acids*, and amino-acids are the carbon compounds which are built into the protein molecules essential to protoplasm. This could have happened during electric storms long ago. If enough of these little chemical building blocks were eventually present in the early earth, atmosphere and sea, sooner or later some would link into more permanent arrangements which might develop the ability to capture carbon compounds from round about and so increase their own size and composition. It sounds simple, but it must have been a very slow and enormously complicated process of evolution. Hundreds of millions of years may have been needed even after the right geological conditions prevailed.

The atmosphere in those far-off days was mostly carbon dioxide, not nitrogen and oxygen as it is now, and it did not shield the earth from the intense ultra-violet radiation from the sun. This kind of solar radiation is harmful to organic materials and perhaps in consequence only in the deeper waters of the sea could complex chemical systems survive which had the ability to grow in a regular way – to reproduce themselves. So far and so much is chemistry. The next steps to produce a living cell from such chemical activity are still far from understood. There may have been many complex arrangements of carbon-containing molecules which did not survive, but at last a carbon-bearing system which enclosed space chemical

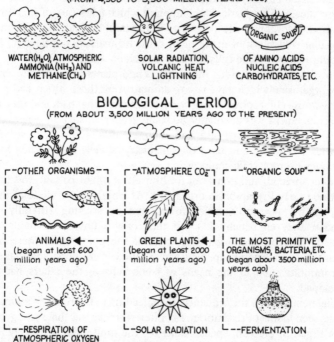

PREBIOLOGICAL PERIOD
(FROM 4,500 TO 3,500 MILLION YEARS AGO)

WATER(H_2O), ATMOSPHERIC AMMONIA (NH_3) AND METHANE(CH_4)

SOLAR RADIATION, VOLCANIC HEAT, LIGHTNING

OF AMINO ACIDS NUCLEIC ACIDS CARBOHYDRATES, ETC.

BIOLOGICAL PERIOD
(FROM ABOUT 3,500 MILLION YEARS AGO TO THE PRESENT)

OTHER ORGANISMS — ATMOSPHERE CO_2 — "ORGANIC SOUP"

ANIMALS (began at least 600 million years ago)

GREEN PLANTS (began at least 2000 million years ago)

THE MOST PRIMITIVE ORGANISMS, BACTERIA, ETC. (began about 3500 million years ago)

RESPIRATION OF ATMOSPHERIC OXYGEN

SOLAR RADIATION

FERMENTATION

Living matter may have evolved from simple chemical compounds long ago by the action of heat, radiation and electrical discharges. When at last cellular organization had been achieved new sources of energy could be used in the increasingly complex chemistry of plants and, later, animals. (After McAlester).

activity could continue with less risk of losing the ions or molecular bits and pieces it required. Foreign, useless or harmful chemicals could be excluded. It was more successful than any previous construction of molecules had been in surviving outside perils. The cell, the essential building brick of organic tissues and the simplest truly living thing, had arrived. It used chemical energy to build more carbon-containing molecules into its structure but it could only keep going if a limited range of chemical and physical conditions existed.

To supplement the 'purely chemical' sources of energy early living matter may have derived some of its strength from an ability to use the energy of sunshine. Plants have long done this with great success in a process called photosynthesis, turning carbon dioxide and water into sugars by this means. The particular compound which takes care of this function is called chlorophyll. It is green, indispensable, and has become the molecular trademark of many plant cells. Animals do not have it. In the Precambrian eon some cells developed such an ability.

How life became divided into animals and plants is not certain, but the early organisms which gave rise to animals were those which had not the ability to use chlorophyll. They ate the organisms that had, and they found the arrangement was adequate. So some groups existed on water, carbon dioxide, a few (nutrient) salts and sunlight; others, unable to survive on such fare, engulfed and used the chemistry of cells that already had the necessary protoplasmic composition.

So far so good, and every cell for himself, it might be said, was the rule for these early Precambrian organisms. At length a new mode of life was adopted by some cells which found that by sticking (literally) close together they all benefited. Until then only a unicellular mode of life existed; multicellular organisms came at the point when there was an advantage in such a link-up. New ways of life became possible and methods of communication of the needs of some cells to the others had to be developed.

The next stage in the sequence, then, leading to the range of animals and plants seen in most Precambrian fossiliferous rocks was that some groups of cells began to perform special tasks for the multi-cellular colony. These cells all had the same structure, forming a *tissue*, and were supported in their activities by other groups of cells which took on different and complementary tasks. By such division of function the entire colony profited. Animals and plants had successfully made the breakthrough into multicellular organization long before the dawn of Cambrian time. As far as we know, however, they were all still confined to the sea or other bodies of water.

Later events which affected the evolution of life on earth have been less difficult to reconstruct or understand. By Cambrian time some animals had the ability to secrete hard protective or supporting (skeletal) parts. In Ordovician times they began to use calcium carbonate in skeletal tissues on an unprecedented scale. Whole new communities of creatures arose as the advantages of hard calcareous 'homes' were made use of. New-found abilities like these (there were others) may have been dependent upon an overall progressive change in the earth's atmosphere by which more and more free oxygen had become available (see page 57). In the shallow seas shell-bearing and other creatures were instrumental in building new environments – shell banks, coral reefs and colonies – places which offered opportunity of food and shelter to many other new forms of life. All the phyla of modern animals had appeared before the Ordovician period was over.

From the sea to fresh water and from water to land were transitions various animals and plants made by Devonian time. Freely available oxygen in the atmosphere enabled a faster production of energy to be made by animals, and the development of vascular tissues (see page 52) in plants helped them colonize the wet landscapes of the day. Rapid evolution followed; ultimately the earth was thoroughly invested with living things, and we must leave the recounting of this to later chapters.

MOLECULAR PALAEONTOLOGY

The word 'fossil' conjures in one's mind the image of a shell, or a bone or a leaf, the common fossils which we may collect on a country ramble or along the sea shore. In recent years, however, another kind of fossil has been collected and studied. This is the (fossil) organic compound which is trapped in sediment when organic matter is buried. As such, of course, it is not a solid hard object that can be hacked out of the rock with a hammer. When in Chapter 3 we examine the geological role of plankton, the myriad floating organisms in the sea, we shall refer to the transformation of the organic matter falling into the sea floor into oil in sedimentary rocks. The oil is a mixture of carbon compounds derived from once-living things. The carbon compounds may include substances unaltered from what they were when forming part of a living organism. They are, in fact, traces of past life and hence are fossils.

Molecular palaeontology is the study of such fossil organic compounds derived from once-living things. The surprising thing is that most sedimentary rocks have some traces of the incredible numbers of organic compounds that are involved in the chemistry of life. When living things die, their substances tend to disperse, and many of the more complex ones are broken down by bacteria. Others combine with oxygen or water, but a few are hardy enough to keep their distinctive molecular structure intact long after the animal or plant of which they once formed a part has completely disappeared. They may survive as particles within the pore spaces in sedimentary rocks, coating the mineral grains, or lying in solution in the pore-waters. Tiny as the amounts of such organic compounds may be, we have now the means of extracting, analysing and identifying many of them.

Many of those *amino-acids* (see page 39) essential to protoplasm survive decomposition of their parent material and only very slowly break down in

the rocks. Some survive for many millions of years and a few are known
from ancient Precambrian sediments. Knowing how long it may take for
some amino-acids and other organic 'geochemicals' to decompose under
various geological conditions, we may one day be able to use them as a sort
of 'geological clock' much as we use radioactive decay to indicate the age of
certain rocks.

HERE TODAY, GONE TOMORROW

As conditions on earth have altered, so life has modified its many forms in
attempts to strike the right balance and survive. As time and environments
have changed the events of the day may have been too rapid or severe for
some organisms to adapt to them and so these animals or plants have
declined and become extinct. For some organisms extinction apparently
came suddenly by geological standards, others dwindled into oblivion
slowly over many millions of years. Imprisoned in the rocks are the fossils
which tell the story; layer upon layer of sedimentary rock takes us from
one moment of geological time to another. As each sediment layer was
deposited the life of the time left its remnants as fossils within the sediments.

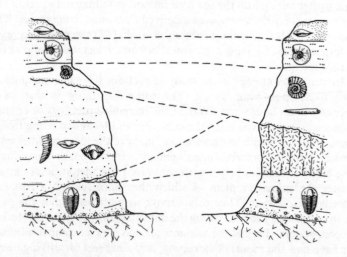

Correlation by fossils. The matching of separated outcrops of rocks by
reference to the fossils they contain is a practice the geologist relies upon
very heavily. In this way complicated geological histories can be discovered.

Wherever we find strata exposed in depth we normally expect to find the first-formed, the oldest of them, at the bottom and the youngest at the top. This arrangement was noted by William Smith, a civil engineer, two hundred years ago, and he put forward the idea that the order of the strata gave an order to the distribution of fossils there; the oldest at the bottom and the youngest at the top. The next step was to deduce that each assemblage of fossils may be unique to that particular time of rock formation, different from those above and below. Within a few decades enough of the geology of Britain, Europe and North America had been examined and sufficient fossils collected to show that between the Precambrian and the present there is a virtually unbroken succession of fossils to mark every moment of geological time. Each span of time has had its own characteristic organisms and has left its own special species of fossils. By using the various fossils as 'date stamps' or emblems of geological age, geologists are able to correlate rocks from one area to another.

In the early days of geology there seemed to the geologists in Europe to be two levels within the rock succession at which there appeared to be great differences between the fossils above and those below. The first or oldest level separated fossils which we now call *Palaeozoic* from those we know as *Mesozoic*; this we noted (pp. 22-23) when recounting the origin of the stratigraphic column. Higher up, the Mesozoic forms are succeeded abruptly by fossils as different again and more closely akin to modern organisms. These are *Cainozoic* forms. So widespread are these abrupt changes and accompanied by so many signs of geological upheaval and change that some eighteenth- and early nineteenth-century geologists thought that they represented universal catastrophies when life was wiped out. By some unexplained means the earth's surface was thereafter suddenly repopulated with animals and plants. This catastrophist view was dispelled by the growth of evidence of the essential continuity of the record of life and geological events was gradually realized. To replace the catastrophists' ideas came those of Charles Darwin, Charles Lyell and others who advocated a theory of evolution. Darwin's book *The Origin of Species*, published in 1859, caused a furore when it advocated evolution by natural selection. Subsequent work has only served to support Darwin's ideas and although we are still puzzled by the apparently sudden extinction of many kinds of life at the close of the Palaeozoic era and again at the end of the Mesozoic we believe that later animals and plants could have originated only from the survivors from the previous geological age.

Fossils add an immensely valuable chapter to the story of evolution. Time and again they have provided clues as to how different groups of organisms have originated and how life has responded to environmental pressures and change. We shall refer to parts of this story many times in the pages that follow.

Not all forms of life have evolved at the same rate. Some fossils appear briefly in the record and others are to be encountered throughout great thicknesses of rock. The fossils most useful to the geologist are often those with the more restricted vertical range – their distribution represents a shorter period of time.

Even on the basis of these fossils we cannot say directly how old a rock is in terms of years. We can only say which period it belongs to. For an idea of age in terms of years we must resort to radiometric methods where possible.

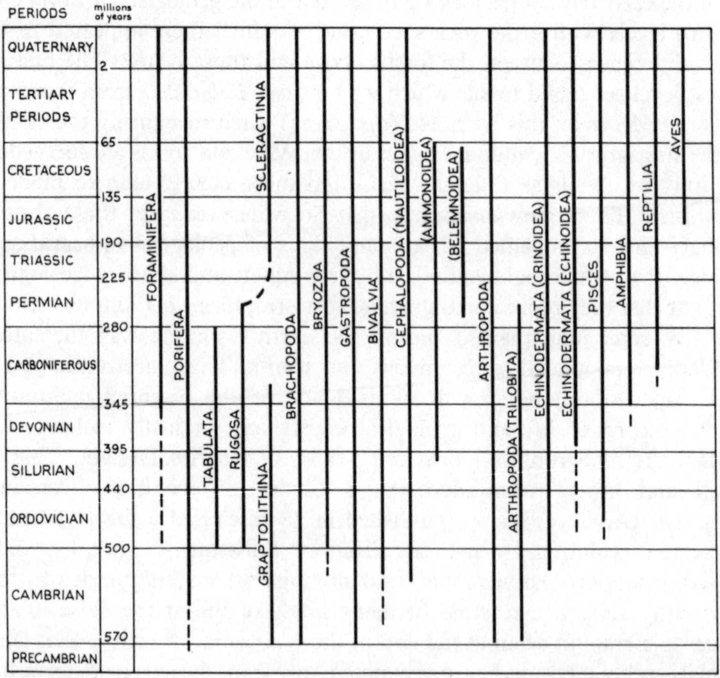
PERIODS
millions of years
QUATERNARY
2
TERTIARY PERIODS
65
CRETACEOUS
135
JURASSIC
190
TRIASSIC
225
PERMIAN
280
CARBONIFEROUS
345
DEVONIAN
395
SILURIAN
440
ORDOVICIAN
500
CAMBRIAN
570
PRECAMBRIAN
FORAMINIFERA
PORIFERA
TABULATA
RUGOSA
SCLERACTINIA
GRAPTOLITHINA
BRACHIOPODA
BRYOZOA
GASTROPODA
BIVALVIA
CEPHALOPODA (NAUTILOIDEA)
(AMMONOIDEA)
(BELEMNOIDEA)
ARTHROPODA
ARTHROPODA (TRILOBITA)
ECHINODERMATA (CRINOIDEA)
ECHINODERMATA (ECHINOIDEA)
PISCES
AMPHIBIA
REPTILIA
AVES

Fossils can be used to identify the particular geological period in which the rock containing them was formed. The geological ranges of most of the major animal groups extend back, however, a mere 500–600 million years.

It has often been said that the fate of all species in the end is extinction and that extinction does exert an influence upon the patterns of living things spread across the world over the ages. In brief, extinction of a species, just as of an individual, occurs when that animal or plant species can no longer cope with its surroundings and the other living things about it. Environmental changes that lead to this sad state of affairs may be physical, chemical or biological. For example, the climate may become too cold, the sea become too salty, the predators too voracious for comfort, for reproduction and, eventually, for life itself. The time at which a fossil species becomes extinct is commonly very hard to establish and the reasons for the extinction are usually even more difficult to fix. We have to be satisfied with approximations for the most part.

However, as we have already noted, there were some occasions in the history of life when extinctions happened in seemingly great numbers, affecting different kinds of organisms within small periods of time. What could be the reason for such events – or 'catastrophes' as some scientists of the last century would have said?

The reasons put forward for such mass extinctions have included volcanic eruptions, climatic changes, cosmic radiation, changes in the earth's magnetic field, epidemic diseases, changes in sea level, changes in the composition of the atmosphere and several other factors. Clearly quite a few of these may be related and there may have been times in the history of the earth when as we shall discuss in Chapter 6, the spread of lands and seas over the face of the planet did change drastically. Other geological factors such as the magnetic field and the composition of the atmosphere could be important in shielding life from the destructive ultraviolet and other radiation from the sun.

It really seems best not to look to any single factor in trying to account for mass extinctions. There must have been an interplay between the various biological factors that determine the existence of species, and this is very difficult to recognize. Factors causing the extinction of a group of plants may thus ultimately deprive animal species of those plants as food and so bring about a second extinction: The whole ecological web may be disrupted and many species ultimately suffer. The fossil record contains innumerable such hints and suggestions but very few certainties about the disappearance of virtually all forms of life of the past.

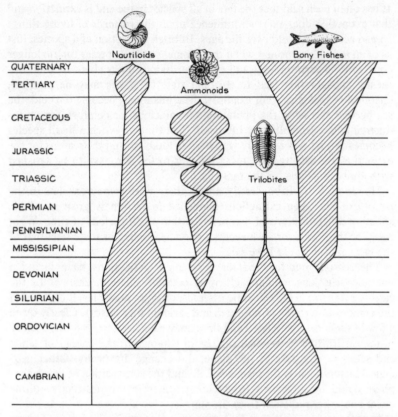

Certain parts of the geological column have, characteristically, abundances of certain kinds of fossils. This abundance seems to diminish in some cases as it grows in others. The shaded columns in this figure indicate in their widths the abundance of different kinds of molluscs, trilobites and fish. Perhaps the extinction of one major kind (for example, trilobites) is brought about by the activities of one or several other kinds. Palaeontologists have to beware that they do not draw hasty and wrong conclusions from greatly simplified diagrams such as this. (After Newell).

FOSSILS AND ENVIRONMENTS

Collecting fossils is, like many things, easier when one knows where to go and what to look for. The best fossil sea-urchins, for example, may be found in chalky limestones and the best graptolites in shiny black shales.

We soon recognize that the distribution of fossils from rock to rock is not a random affair. Certain fossils occur most commonly in certain types of sedimentary rock. We could say that rock lithology seems to control fossil content. It sounds more scientific. What, however, can be said about the actual preferences that the organisms of the past had for the places in which they lived? We recognize that species differ from one another in their food, temperature tolerance, and other requirements. Their distribution is largely controlled by these things and, in the case of aquatic organisms, also by the factors which control the kind of sediment being deposited. Each organism has its *habitat*, the kind of place, or environment, where it lives best. The classification of habitats is usually based on environmental factors that seem to be the most important in determining animal distribution.

The most obvious division of habitats is into aquatic and terrestrial. Aquatic environments include freshwater, marine or brackish, shallow, deep, rocky, tropical, and so on. Most fossils are the remains of marine organisms so we may reasonably confine ourselves to a view of marine environments (figure below). There seems to be little reason for thinking that environments in the ancient seas were very different from those in the seas today, at least insofar as their physical nature was concerned.

Within the ocean, we can also distinguish here different modes of life among the inhabitants of these environments. On the bottom is the *benthos*; floating in the water is the *plankton*; swimming by is the *nekton*. The benthos may be preserved in the place where it dies, but the *pelagic* or free organisms have to fall to the bottom before they can become fossils. As corpses they may drift far from where normally they would have lived.

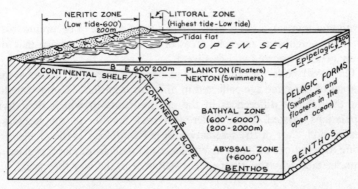

Most of the organisms that may become fossils live in the sea where they may float or swim (plankton, nekton) or live on the bottom (benthos).

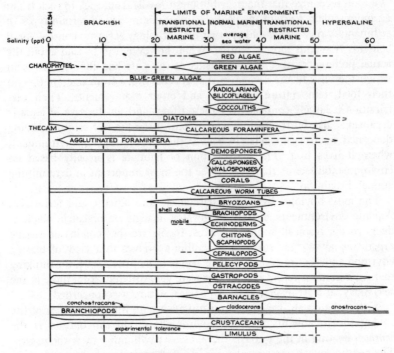

Invertebrate animals and the simplest plants today are relatively restricted to either life on land or life in the sea. Here their ranges across the various environments is shown. This kind of information can help the geologist interpret the rocks in which such fossils occur. (After Heckel).

Benthonic animals in sandy areas stand a good chance of becoming fossils, but their neighbours in rocky areas or in the open sea above may only rarely become interred and fossilized.

The fossil collector, then, may recognize differences between fossil samples of the same age collected in different localities. He may conclude that they reflect differences in the environments in which their living populations existed. Some differences may be due to the hazards of preservation. Part of the fascination in palaeontology is the challenge of trying to recognize different assemblages of fossils from place to place and to understand why the groups are distributed in the way they are.

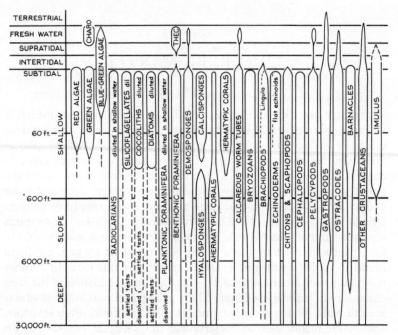

Many modern simple plants and creatures are relatively restricted to waters of definite depth and salinity. Fossils can be used tentatively to suggest the depth (and salinity) of the water in which the sediment enclosing them was deposited. Hermatypic corals are those that form reefs; ahermatypic do not. *Limulus* is the king-crab. (After Heckel).

CHAPTER 2

THE GREEN MANTLE

WITHOUT plant life the world would be a desert and the history of its surface would have been very different. The air we breathe contains a supply of oxygen which is continuously replenished by photosynthesis, the chemical activity of green plants utilizing sunlight to convert carbon dioxide from the air into carbohydrates. To burn petrol in cars, oil in industry, and even just to keep more and more people alive, we need an adequate and increasing supply of oxygen. One of the worries that have been expressed in these days of so much atmospheric pollution is that the plant kingdom may not be able to keep pace with modern man's excessive demand for oxygen, but there seems to be little scientific evidence to support this idea. In another way too, plants are indispensable – they are the foundation of the food chain for the animal kingdom. Their protoplasm and other products are the basic food sources for animals. And in subtle, often invisible, ways some plants such as bacteria and fungi help in breaking down dead matter into simpler substances more useful to other organisms.

What a diverse collection of living things is to be included in the plant kingdom; but most of them can be grouped under a few well-known headings – algae, fungi, bacteria, mosses, ferns, conifers and flowering plants. Classifications are basically matters of convenience, and the list just mentioned is not too different from the kind of classification most generally used by botanists. It may help if to begin our discussion of the role that plants play in the natural economy of the surface of the earth we list a few of the attributes plants share with animals. These are cellular organizations, metabolic processes, sexual reproduction, genetic phenomena, and adaptation. It is the ways in which these attributes are brought together to produce a living organism which perhaps should be our basis for classification. Leaving aside, however, all the divisions which figure in the various botanic classifications and excluding the bacteria, we can group living plants simply as follows:

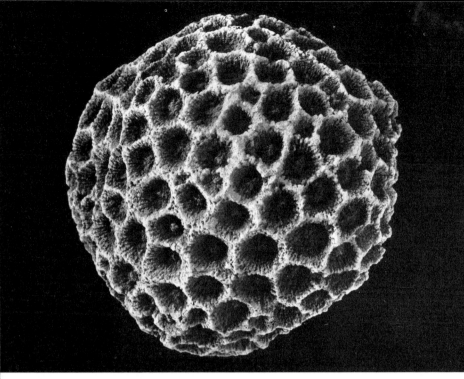

PLATE 3. *Above*, a small colony of the rugose coral *Michelinia* (× 1.5) viewed from above. *Below*, *Halysites* (× 1), the tabulate 'chain coral', seen from above.

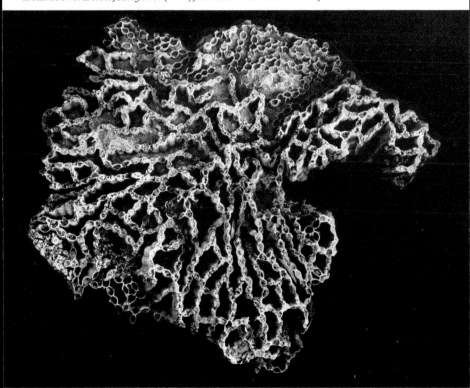

PLATE 4. *Right*, fragments of segmented scorpion-like eurypterids such as these occur in rocks of Silurian and Devonian rocks ($\times$ 1). *Below*, trace fossils commonly are not what they seem at first sight: this is the infilled feeding burrow of an unknown creature, not a fossil snake. It comes from early Palaeozoic rocks which are vastly older than the oldest snake ($\times$ 0.5).

Common name	Approximate number of species
Algae	19,000
Fungi	42,000
Liverworts	9,000
Mosses	14,000
Club mosses and horsetails	1,100
Ferns	9,500
Maidenhair tree	1
Conifers	550
Flowering plants	250,000
Approximate total	350,000

These different groups show an enormous range of evolutionary development, with the simplest of them appearing early in the geological record and the more highly evolved coming later. For example, fossil algae are found in rocks more than a thousand million years old, but flowering plants are not known from rocks earlier than Cretaceous, about a hundred million years old.

THE ALGAE

Pond scum and seaweeds and even some 'mosses' are all typical algae, even though at first sight they may have little in common. To the botanist they are chlorophyll-bearing organisms with unicellular or multicellular sex organs in which every cell may develop into a new individual. Geologically, they have a long and important history.

Algae need water. They can live not only in the sea, fresh water and in the soil; they also grow on moist stones, wood, and even in or on certain other plants and animals. They are the producers of energy-rich compounds which are needed by so many other living things. Planktonic (floating) plants are tremendously important in this way and it is thought that nearly 90 per cent of the photosynthesis on earth is carried on by the planktonic algae. Although most algae use atmospheric carbon dioxide in their metabolism, some forms of blue-green algae and some bacteria take nitrogen from the atmosphere to build into their protoplasm. This *nitrogen fixation* significantly adds nitrogenous compounds to the soil and water where the plants live. Other plants can then readily make use of these materials in their own metabolism.

Man uses algae as food and for many other purposes. He may take algal 'gardens' with him on long space flights in the future to use up

F. D

his waste products and turn them back into substances he can use for food himself.

Not all algae are useful or even pleasant; many appear or smell offensive. When the conditions in nature are favourable algae may arise in great concentrations, turning water green or red in a 'water bloom'. They poison the water with their wastes and the decomposition of dead algae depletes the oxygen. Fish die and the water is fouled. Enormous algal growth has taken place in recent years in ponds and reservoirs where fertilizers have been washed in from farmers' fields and the once clear waters grow green and scummy. Effluents from sewage works are often rich in the compounds that promote algal growth. This happens especially where the bacteria used to break down raw sewage cannot cope with the immense quantities the sewage works have to handle. Algae range from minute unicellular species through hair-like and other simple forms to large complex plants such as kelp, 'sea lettuce' and bladder-wrack. Some may be globular colonial masses, others interwoven meshworks of fibres. Many have a rather complex reproductive cycle.

The *blue-green* algae may have a distinctive colour and their species are widely distributed. Most of them are unicellular or colonial or small filamentous forms. *Green* algae are similarly widespread but are predominant in fresh water. The common red or brown seaweeds belong to the exclusively marine *brown* algae, and include the largest algal plants known. Some *red* algae are freshwater inhabitants, but most are marine and a few are very beautiful.

Many algae are unicellular flagellate organisms and more than a few of them, the *diatoms*, impregnate their cell walls with silica to make a delicate skeleton which persists after the death of the plant. *Diatomaceous earth* is the silicous mud which accumulates on the floor of bodies of water where diatoms thrive.

BACTERIA, SLIME MOULDS AND FUNGI

Bacteria seem to be the simplest and most minute living organisms with cellular organization. The smallest of them may be as little as half a micron (0.001 mm is a micron) in width! They are typical of the organisms described in this section, many of which lack chlorophyll and are dependent for materials to build their bodies upon the complex substances made by the green plants. Many of them break down complex organic substances into carbon dioxide and water. A few bacteria can synthesize their protoplasm from inorganic compounds

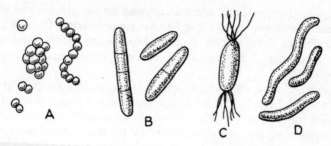

Some different kinds of bacteria (A–D), which are perhaps the world's most numerous organisms. Fossil bacteria from Precambrian formations have been identified (with some difficulty) and are among the world's oldest fossils. The role of bacteria in the history of life on earth is hard to assess but it must have been very important. (After Bold).

by using the chemical energy released when these compounds are oxidized. Iron and copper sulphide ores provide certain bacteria with such a source of energy, and the oxides that result can be collected as an economic product. It seems odd to use bacteria as mineral extractors, but an increasing amount of research is being done to breed 'ore-hungry' bacteria.

We commonly think of bacteria as food-spoiling or disease-causing organisms, but many of their activities are beneficial to man. There is a large flora of these organisms in the human intestine.

Like algae, bacteria are found in ancient rocks. Precambrian formations at least 1200 million years old in Canada and Africa have preserved bacterial bodies. A truly remarkable instance of preservation has been found in Permian salt where the bacteria were still alive.

The *slime moulds* are a problematic group of organisms sometimes thought to be 'animal-like plants' or 'plant-like animals', depending on whether one is a zoologist or a botanist. Certainly they are primitive in organization and in their life histories resemble both fungi and protozoa. The geologist, however, has been able to find no trace of them as fossils, nor does he see them as organisms that contribute much to the geological cycle.

Fungi cannot be dismissed quite so briefly; although they are not exactly abundant as fossils, they are known from several rocks where an unusual chance preservation has occurred. The fungi are familiar to us as mushrooms and toadstools, but these are not really very typical of the vast numbers of fungi known. Unicellular and multicellular, aquatic and non-aquatic types occur, and for the greater part of their existence they may be quite unlike the spore-bearing 'fruiting bodies' we collect in damp woods or fields. Moulds and yeasts, mildews and lichens, should all be considered as fungi, some pleasant, some un-pleasant.

Together with the bacteria and some algae, the fungi help break down dead bodies and discarded organic materials. Without their activity, the surface of the earth would soon have become smothered by corpses of one sort or another. In fossilization, as we saw, the preservation of soft tissues is very rare and in fact only occurs where the corpse-devouring organisms have been prevented from clearing up.

Fungal filaments and traces are, nevertheless, known from some very fine-grained sediments. The Precambrian Gunflint Formation chert has several kinds of fungi preserved in it, and from many later rocks fungi have been recorded. These plants must have been very common in the great forest swamps of the Carboniferous period.

MOSSES AND LIVERWORTS

Land plants and animals appear later in the geological record than aquatic forms. Land plants are thought to have evolved from aquatic ancestors, and two contrasting kinds have developed. In the *vascular* plants is a tissue which conducts food and water from one part of the organism to another. Vascular tissue is tough, useful material. Plants that lack it, the *non-vascular*, are generally small and moisture-loving, primitive in structure and familiar as the mosses and liverworts.

Mosses consist of a slender leafy axis, either erect or prostrate, and absorptive 'rootlets'. They rarely occur as single individuals but form extensive colonies on moist soil, rock or wood. Mosses growing on soil help to bind it together and prevent erosion. Many mosses have been geologically preserved or 'petrified' because they have grown in water where evaporation on the surface of the plants has caused the precipitation of calcium carbonate in a form known as tufa.

Peat or bog mosses are important geologically because they help the soil to hold water and increase the acidity of soils even when dead.

Liverworts are small plants, so-called because they look in some cases like the lobes of an animal liver. They like wet conditions and are fairly widespread. The reason for this lies partly in their lack of vascular tissues. Pride of place everywhere has gone to the vascular plants. The liverworts are a long way behind the mosses and vascular plants when it comes to adapting to drier conditions. Liverworts are known from the Carboniferous rocks in Europe and North America and must have thrived in the coal swamp forests (see p. 58).

FERNS, CLUB MOSSES AND HORSETAILS

The next group to mention is a large one of spore-producing vascular plants, and of these the *ferns* are the most conspicuous today. Among the extinct Devonian flora there were several vascular plants, the Psilophytes, that lacked both leaves and roots. They have been found well preserved in chert in Scotland.

A little farther back in the Palaeozoic era the *club* and *spike 'mosses'*

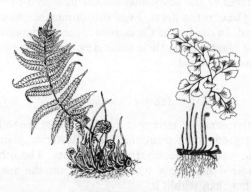

Ferns are known from rocks as old as the Devonian. They always seem to have liked damp places. (After H. C. Bold).

must have originated and spread out across the land. They have been called 'mosses' because living members of the group look rather like mosses. The 'club' and 'spike' names refer to their spore-bearing structures. *Lycopodium* is the common club-moss found in many damp habitats in Britain. It is a small plant and seems to be a very puny descendant of the great Carboniferous species.

The *horsetail ferns* are another group of once-prolific primitive vascular plants represented by a mere handful of species today. *Equisetum* is the common horsetail (p. 62) with whorls of little bladelike leaves arranged at intervals along the stem. Spores are produced in the terminal sporangia.

True ferns are a diverse series of plants, nearly all of which like damp conditions. Some are large-leaved erect forms growing in forests; some are aquatic. The spore-producing organs are usually situated on the surface of the leaves. And in the ferns the leaves are proportionally rather large.

Botanists, being human, tend to disagree about the classification of the groups of vascular plants just described. The geological evidence suggests that the ferns, club-mosses, liverworts and mosses all had separate origins in Silurian or earlier times. Throughout Palaeozoic days these plants had a virtually unchallenged role on the face of the earth. But beginning in the Carboniferous period they were gradually replaced by conifers and other seed-bearing plants. Seeds enable plants to reproduce successfully in dry environments. Late in the Palaeozoic era the advantages of the adaptation led the new seed-producers into the dominant place in the floras. Even this dominance was eventually to be challenged. In the Lower Cretaceous rocks are the earliest known fossil flowering plants. From these same new arrivals sprang the great floras of the modern world.

SEED PLANTS

Amongst the thousands of seed-bearing plants there are today the two clearly distinct groups just mentioned. The flowering plants – *angiosperms* – house seeds in special structures, fruits. The other group – the *gymnosperms* – has seeds which develop on the surface of an appendage rather than within it.

The gymnosperms are woody, being either trees, shrubs or vines. Pine trees are the common typical forms but one or two oddities from the past, such as the cycad trees and the maidenhair tree, *Ginkgo*, are other members of the group.

The flowering plants include not only woody types like oak trees, roses and heathers but also soft herbaceous kinds such as buttercups, daisies, grasses, and so on. Without these the world would be less colourful and man would have to look elsewhere for an immense number of materials and foods. No other group of vascular plants exceeds the flowering kinds in range and diversity of plant body and habitat.

Indeed, seed plants are so common, important and well known a category of plants that we will say no more about their biology at this point.

Some of the oldest fossils known are undoubtedly plants, though of a very simple kind. From Devonian time onwards, however, the vascular plants have left abundant traces of their history, and palaeobotany enables us to visualize the background against which many of the animals of the geological past must be set. Plant remains contribute not only to our understanding of the evolution of the plant kingdom and of the environments of the past, they also help us in problems of geological correlation, just as animal fossils do. One particular kind of vegetable structure, the spore or pollen grain, seems to be especially useful in this connection.

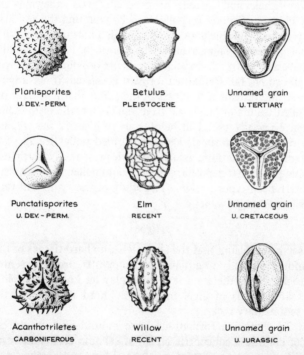

Planisporites
U. DEV.- PERM.

Betulus
PLEISTOCENE

Unnamed grain
U. TERTIARY

Punctatisporites
U. DEV. – PERM.

Elm
RECENT

Unnamed grain
U. CRETACEOUS

Acanthotriletes
CARBONIFEROUS

Willow
RECENT

Unnamed grain
U. JURASSIC

Spores and pollen grains are very small but they are relatively tough and withstand fossilization very well. These are common examples from various geological formations some of which have very distinctive and characteristic assemblages of spores or pollen. Unfortunately it is a long and difficult business to extract these beautiful tiny structures from the rock. Magnified approximately 35 times.

Although most plant tissues decompose very rapidly under normal conditions, spores and pollen cells are remarkably resistant. Being of microscopic proportions and carried afar by wind and water, they are transported into all manner of places where deposition of sediment goes on, even far out at sea. In the last few decades these tiny objects have been recovered in vast numbers from sedimentary rocks as old as Silurian. They have proved to be of real value in correlating rocks in many parts of the world and of many different ages. Recovering such fossils is a difficult business which involves dissolving the rock in hydruofloric acid and searching the residue with a powerful microscope. When rock samples are treated in this way – shales and siltstones are especially good – they may yield very rich assemblages of spores or pollen and by counting the various species in a sample a recognizable flora may be found. This does not mean that the individual species of plant can always be identified. For species alive today we can have a recognizable association of spore or pollen with leaves, stem, flowers and so on, but for extinct forms it is difficult if not impossible to relate these microfossils with pieces of the plants that may have produced them. Pollen counts or 'analyses' from muds and silts of the Quaternary have been especially useful in helping us to identify the climate under which a deposit was formed. Deposits formed under ice-age conditions have assemblages like those associated with present-day northland floras, interglacial phases left deposits with pores and pollen from temperate land or Mediterranean types of flora. The study of these tiny but very useful fossils is known as palynology.

Algae

It may seem surprising that the algae, with no hard tissues of their own and confined virtually to aquatic environments, are represented at all in the rocks. Nevertheless a few algae play an important role as rock builders and fossils of algal origin are found in some of the most ancient sedimentary rocks.

Many Precambrian formations have mound-like structures which consist of countless concentric layers of calcium carbonate resembling those built by modern blue-green algae. These *stromatolites* may reach several metres in diameter and were probably formed in the marine tidal zone. Certain algae in tropical coastal areas produce a sticky surface of filaments to which coral- or lime-sand grains adhere. As the filaments grow upwards new grains are trapped and a mound-like body is constructed. Other algae seem to produce calcium carbonate as part of their metabolic activity, and various distinctive little structures result from this. Not the least important part played by some such algal

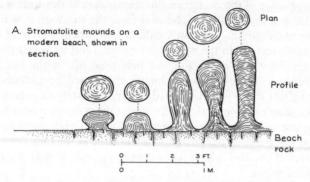

A. Stromatolite mounds on a modern beach, shown in section.

Plan

Profile

Beach rock

Calcareous algae and stromatolites. Some algae deposit a thin film of calcium carbonate on parts of their surface. Others bind together lime-sand in a meshwork of tiny sticky threads. In each case the result may be a mass of limestone. Stromatolites are such layered lumps or masses. They grow today on tropical lagoon beaches and in other carbonate-rich sea waters. Fossil stromatolites up to 2 m (7 ft) high are known; and examples come from some of the oldest fossiliferous rocks, where they occur in thousands.

growths is that of cementing together the shells, coral colonies and other pieces of organic hardware on the sea floor. Many a coral reef consists in large part of algal calcium carbonate.

Algae form an extremely important part of the plankton, and the role these plants have there is described in Chapter 3.

Another role some algae play is that of boring tiny holes into shells and other calcareous structures. By so doing they may destroy a lot of otherwise fossilizable material or create spaces which become filled by non-organic matter.

Algae and Atmosphere

In Precambrian times the atmosphere was probably oxygen-poor. Only organisms that could manage without oxygen were much in evidence. The algae, however, by their photosynthetic activities, began to produce local concentrations of oxygen. Ultimately there was more than enough oxygen produced to satisfy inorganic chemical processes in the crust. Free oxygen began to accumulate in the atmosphere. By 600 million years ago, at the end of the Precambrian eon, there may have been enough oxygen produced everywhere to support animal respiration.

A consequence of the change in the atmosphere at this time was that the intense and deadly ultra-violet rays from the sun were now filtered out of the atmosphere. The sun's radiation produces a layer of ozone (O_3) from the oxygen in the upper atmosphere, and its harmful effects are dispersed by this layer. For the first time life in the sea found oxygen ready to use and was no longer threatened by radiation. By Devonian times the oxygen increased to approximately its present level and life became possible on the land without the protection of radiation-shielding water. The forests that grew in Carboniferous times not only continued the trend of oxygen-enrichment, but as we shall see below, have provided the fuel which we so busily recombine with oxygen in our modern world.

Liverworts and Mosses

So fragile are these plants that they are rarely preserved. The coal seams of the Carboniferous formations have yielded a few examples and scattered instances of them have been found in later formations. We can ignore them here.

Coal Swamp Floras

The club mosses, the horsetails, and other seedless vascular plants are well known from coal seam fossils and early forms have been found in the Devonian Rhynie cherts in Scotland. Similar plants and club mosses are known in Silurian rocks as are some doubtful specimens from the Cambrian. Their interest lies in the fact that they are land plants, but more impressive and important is the great outburst of tree plants that began in the middle Devonian. These and the horse-tails flourished as some of the principal members of the great Carboniferous swamp forests.

The seed-bearing plants joined them in profusion in the Carboniferous. Coal seams are the compressed and carbonized remains of the plants that lived, died and fell to the ground in the vast swampy areas of those days. From the coals and from the black shales that overlie them one can often obtain splendidly preserved pieces of bark or impressions of leaves or roots or even trunks of these plants. The largest plants of the coal forests were seed ferns as much as 30 m high. The Carboniferous swamp on p. 62, and the figure on p. 59 shows some of the commonest British Carboniferous plant fossils. If one calculates that it takes 20 m of plant debris to make 1 m of coal, the thickest coal

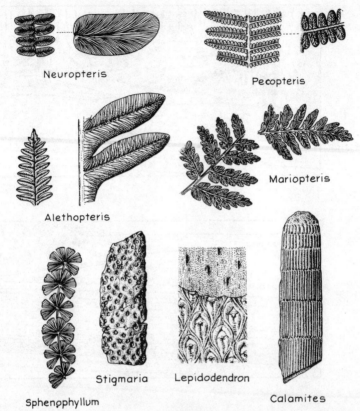

Neuropteris

Pecopteris

Mariopteris

Alethopteris

Sphenophyllum

Stigmaria

Lepidodendron

Calamites

Some fossil plants from the Carboniferous rocks are clearly related to the ferns. Other fossils are less easily recognizable parts of the roots, bark or trunks of other plants. (About half natural size; after *British Palaeozoic Fossils*).

seams known, over 75 m thick, represent a truly immense amount of plant debris. Modern plants accumulate today in swampy areas to give peat at a rate of perhaps 0.5 m (20 ins) in ten years.

The transformation of the vegetable matter into coal involves chemical and physical changes. Moisture and volatile constituents are squeezed out and the remaining molecules are rearranged. What remains is very largely composed of hydrocarbons (compounds of carbon and hydrogen). Unlike many minerals, coal has no fixed and definite chemical composition. Hydrocarbons are of many different

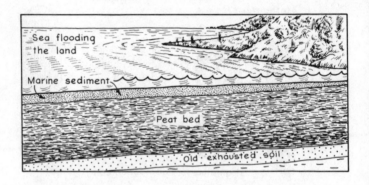

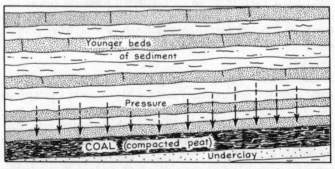

Coal is formed from the vegetable matter that accumulates in swampy areas. Compression transforms soft spongy peat into a much thinner band or seam of hard, compact and brittle coal.

types, and coals are mixtures of several of these. What is essential in the conversion of plant matter to coal is the removal of oxygen. Bacteria are amongst the more important agencies in this conversion because they break down the complex carbohydrates in the plants into simpler stable compounds.

The kinds of plants originally present are important in controlling the type of coal to be produced – they are the biological ingredients. Depth of burial, time, and possibly heat and dynamic or regional metamorphism also control the kind of coal that results. These factors are involved in processing the vegetable matter through a series of changes that reduce the proportions of oxygen and hydrogen present and increase the proportion of carbon. The *rank* of the coal – lignitic, bituminous, anthracitic, etc. – indicates the degree to which these changes have taken place.

Peat is matted plant debris in various stages of decomposition. It is black, porous, woody, or fibrous.

Lignite (brown coal) is a little more altered from the original state than peat. It is brownish black and may look rather like stiff cardboard.

Bituminous coal usually has a laminated structure with the layers having different lustres. It is black, dull to shining, and has a roughly cubic fracture. Individually identifiable pieces of plant are rare. Bituminous coal contains sooty layers which leave a mark on paper.

Anthracite is a hard, black, lustrous coal, brittle and breaking with a conchoidal fracture. It will not soil paper. Being the most altered plant matter, it contains a very high proportion of carbon and burns with a short blue flame, giving off little smoke.

Most of the seams in the British coalfields are of bituminous coal, but some seams in the west of the South Wales coalfields and parts of the northern coalfields are of anthracite. The tip heaps in many coalfields have yielded plenty of splendid fossil plants. In the smooth black shales associated with the seams themselves, leaves, fronds and entire plants may be found. Sandstones may have fossil wood, tree stumps, trunks and roots. Some very large specimens may still be found in the sandstones of the Coal Measures. Under the coal seams pale clays may occur. These are in some cases 'fossil' soils, and one can still find traces and fossils of the large and small roots that the coal plants sent down into the ground. Other clays contain nodules which may have plant remains beautifully preserved within them.

A coal swamp forest. The various plants shown in the Fig. on p. 59 would
have been abundant in such a forest.

Angiosperms and the Mesozoic Floras

In some parts of the world there are extensive coal swamp deposits of
Mesozoic age, and in Britain the Mesozoic plants left a good record of their
existence. Although Triassic plants are relatively rare everywhere, there
are Jurassic coals at Brora in Scotland, and in Yorkshire there are fossil
plant beds with many beautiful specimens. The early Mesozoic rocks of
southern and central Britain have a few plant remains and in the Wealden
(Cretaceous) beds of the south-east and south fossil 'horsetails' are well
known.

Perhaps the 'fossil forest' at Lulworth Cove is one of the most famous
of the Mesozoic fossil plant localities in Britain. There the stems and
boles of cycad trees are preserved in silica and covered in deposits of
tufa (a porous limey deposit).

The most important botanical event in Mesozoic times, however, was
the arrival of the flowering plants. Their exact origins are still hotly debated,
but in early Cretaceous rocks the group is clearly present. From Cretaceous
times onwards most floras have included flowering plants; deciduous trees
and grasses have spread to change the whole aspect of the landscape.

Plants in the dry and desert landscape of Europe in Triassic times.

CAINOZOIC FOSSIL PLANTS

Throughout Cainozoic time there was no really spectacular change in the floras of the world until the great cooling events of the Ice Age. The distribution of fossil Cainozoic animals, and more especially of Cainozoic plants, suggests that vegetation was less subject to climatic differences from one part of the world to another than it is today. During the last few million years, however, the climate has suffered severe changes and the belts of different kinds of vegetation moved equatorwards in response.

One cannot help feeling also that the Cainozoic floras must have had more than a little influence upon the evolution of the land mammals and the birds. Without grassy plains would there have evolved the many swift-running mammals that are now found there? Did the African forests and savannahs influence the rise of the great apes and perhaps man himself?

From the London Clay and in South Devon and various other localities in southern England we have evidence of Cainozoic floras. The London Clay flora includes over fifty plant families, and hundreds of specimens of leaves, pieces of wood, fruit and seeds have been collected.

The Oligocene lake deposits at Bovey Tracy in South Devon contain lignite and fossils of sequoia and magnolia trees.

Among the sands, clays and gravels that were spread across Britain at the retreat of the great ice sheets a few score thousand years ago are swamp and pond deposits of peat. We can identify in these deposits willow, birch and other trees and plants which today inhabit the colder areas of Europe. Mosses and sedges are present, and in the finest deposits there are also the remains of bugs and beetles that lived in the cold wet tundra.

Around parts of the coast of Britain are some of the most recent fossils or subfossils – the tree stumps and roots of the 'Buried Forest'. At low tides they protrude from the clay and peat that supported them a few thousand years ago. They are a reminder that geological change is a constant and important process influencing life on earth.

Finally we should mention one kind of occurence of plant remains that links animals and plants; it is in *coprolites*, fossil dung, that we have evidence of animals feeding on plants. Some small coprolites have been found in rocks as old as Carboniferous. They are rare, commonly phosphatic objects and most contain animal debris, but those that yield plant material seem to indicate true herbivores. The Carboniferous examples contain spores, sporangia, cuticle and other plant tissue, but what the herbivorous animal was remains unknown. Other examples from Mesozoic and Cainozoic rocks are known from any parts of the world and in the case of the extinct cave-dwelling sloths of the Americas coprolitic material is locally so common that some years ago a mass of it caught fire in a cave and is still burning.

CHAPTER 3

THE VAGRANT HORDES

As we remarked in the first chapter of this book, the earth is a wet planet. Most of its water is gathered into the great oceans, and it was perhaps in the oceans that life itself first began. The seas and oceans not only play a part in the natural economy of the world but are becoming increasingly important in the activities of the ever-growing human population. Each year man needs more natural resources and more food, and for these he is beginning seriously and intensively to explore the seas. Among the harvests that he may directly reap one day is the *plankton* – the myriad floating forms of life, many of them microscopic, which are important food for the fish and larger marine creatures. Plankton includes both free-floating animals and plants, and must have existed in the seas for virtually as long as life itself has existed. Its role in geology as well as in biology is by no means a small one.

In the year 1828 an amateur naturalist hit upon the idea of catching small specimens at sea by towing a fine net behind his vessel. J.

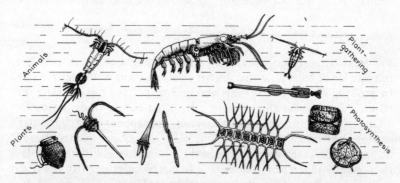

Plankton. The tiny floating plants in the upper layers of the oceans are incredibly abundant. They produce food by photosynthesis and themselves are food for very small animals in the sea. Most of the plants are invisible to the naked eye and the animals can only be examined properly by using a microscope. Some form of plankton seems to have been in the sea since mid-Precambrian time.

Vaughan Thompson was by this means able to collect concentrations of microscopic life floating in the uppermost layers of the sea. It was, however, not until many years later that the study of plankton was taken very seriously. During the mid- and later parts of the nineteenth century it was found that life existed in the great depths of the oceans and that the sediments over much of the deep ocean floor contained countless microscopic shells. Techniques were evolved to collect samples of water and life from every depth, and the distribution of plankton both across the seas and vertically within them slowly became known. This distribution is constantly changing. Tides, currents, temperature, salts and salinity, the seasons and day and night all have their effects upon it.

Included in the plankton are not only genuinely microscopic plants and animals but also the eggs and larvae of many kinds of larger animals. All are affected by geographical and climatic changes, and sudden changes in conditions can be disastrous to plankton and hence to the fishes and others dependent upon planktonic food.

At sea, as on land, the plant kingdom provides much of the animal kingdom with food. The energy of sunlight is used by plants in making the starches, sugars and proteins that animals depend on. More than 99 per cent of all the plants in the sea belong to the microscopic plankton floating in the uppermost 30 m or so of the water where sunlight penetrates. They are called the *phytoplankton*, and the tiny animals associated with them are known as the *zooplankton*.

PHYTOPLANKTON

Far from being of uniform composition throughout, the oceans have in their lower layers a rather higher concentration of the salts needed by growing plants. Land plants obtain from soil the mineral salts they require. In the seas the nutrient salts often rise towards the surface after periods of disturbance of the waters, as happens after the winter's storms. With sunlight to help, the tiny, unicellular plants speedily utilize the minerals, grow and reproduce so that in as little as two days they may double their numbers. The sea is infested with a rapidly multiplying flora. In turn, a veritable epidemic or plague of tiny animals may follow.

Most important of the phytoplankton may be the single-celled algae, the *diatoms* (see p. 67). Each diatom has a transparent intricate case with tiny filaments and spikes projecting, rather like the hairs of thistledown. The case is made of silica extracted from the water.

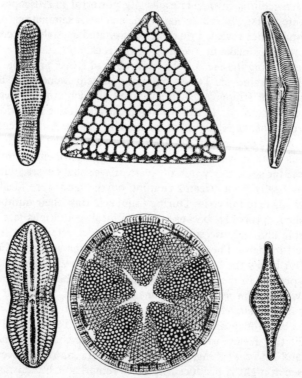

Diatoms. These are unicellular microscopic plants, which live in water and secrete a porous skeleton of silica (opal). Their intricate and beautiful skeletons are of many different shapes. Marine diatoms are abundant in the plankton. Known from Jurassic (rocks) to the present they locally occur in such profusion that they make up formations hundreds of metres thick. Freshwater diatoms are much less common. (Approx. × 100)

Intricate though the pattern of each diatom is, it is clearly a very orderly and symmetrical arrangement. The earliest known diatoms are from Cambrian rocks.

Another important algal member of this community is the group known as *coccolithophores*. These, too, are unicellular, tiny algae which secrete a case or 'skeleton'. In these plants the case is a sphere composed of many round platelets or discs. Each disc or coccolith is made of crystalline calcium carbonate and has a distinctive pattern of ornamentation and perforations. Not until comparatively recently were we able to study coccoliths in detail; especially powerful microscopes had to be invented first. By these same means, an examination of many chalky limestones revealed that not precipitated crystals but coccoliths in vast numbers make up the bulk of the rock.

Contemplating the *chalk* in the white cliffs of Dover or on the Downs, or in the Ukraine or Texas, one cannot help wondering how the Cretaceous seas supported such an incredibly rich crop of these algae. It has left behind one of the world's most distinctive and widespread rock formations, as much as 500 m thick in places. And coccoliths are perhaps only 0.001 mm in diameter! The reason may be that because of various earth movements great areas of the continents were flooded by the sea for some thirty million years. These shallow seas with a flow of mineral salts from streams running off the land were ideal for the coccolith algae to thrive in. During Cainozoic time their numbers have diminished, probably because geographical conditions are not so favourable and because some creatures have developed an insatiable appetite for them. The earliest known coccoliths are from Cambrian rocks, but below the late Mesozoic formations few are known.

Also present in the plankton are some odd in-between creatures or plants which seem to be neither one nor the other. They are the unicellular *dinoflagellates*. Dinoflagellates have a skin or case of cellulose and are able to manufacture their own food, just like plants. They also use their tiny feelers to beat their way through the water and to entangle and eat other things, as do animals. The phosphorescence seen in the sea at night is produced by these remarkable organisms.

When conditions are ripe and nutrient salts are available in quantity, the dinoflagellates may suddenly multiply very rapidly. They use up the available oxygen in the sea and pollute the water with their waste products and dead bodies in what is commonly called a 'red tide'. 'Red tides' are usually disastrous to other forms of life in the sea. Fish are poisoned by the million and a rain of dead organisms falls to the sea floor.

It is thought that dinoflagellates may have been the cause of remarkable mass mortalities in the seas of the past. Some fossiliferous sedimentary rocks may hold the victims of 'red tides' as abundant fish fossils and other well-preserved remains.

Clearly, in the event of these 'tides' a great deal of organic matter is produced and one way or another may find its way into the sediment on the sea floor and into solutions in the waters just above the floor. Some of this material may contribute to the production of *petroleum* (see p. 81).

With so much food available as phytoplankton it is no wonder that a menagerie of zooplankton has evolved to feed upon it. No one really knows yet how many different kinds of creatures may be drifting and swimming around in the plankton. Every major kind of animal, every phylum in the classification, from unicellular types, the protozoa, to fish of all kinds, is represented in it. To emphasize the enormous production of living things in the planktonic layers of the sea, an

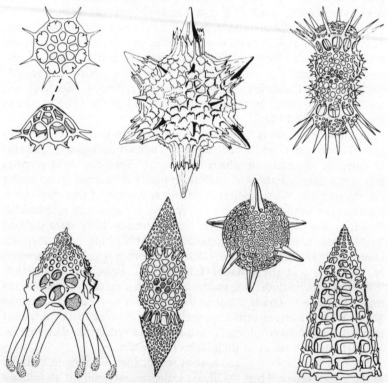

Radiolaria are protozoa, unicellular animals, that secrete coarsely porous skeletons of silica. In this they resemble the diatoms. They are, however, confined to the sea and to ancient marine sediments. They swim near the surface of the water. No radiolaria are known for certain in rocks older than Devonian, but they have been reported from rocks thought to be Precambrian. (All very greatly enlarged)

American scientist not long ago calculated that young blue whales in the Antarctic eat about three tons of tiny shrimps, called krill, every 24 hours. The blue whale seems, however, to feed only during six months of the year, which means that over 500 tons of krill are gulped down by each whale per year. Before the whaling ships came, there were enough blue whale in the Antarctic to put away 270 million tons of krill a year. Despite the whale's appetite, the krill survived from year to year. It is possible that each year some 1100 trillion krill are spawned annually, and krill is only one kind of zooplankton.

Several groups of zooplankton have hard cases, skeletons or *tests*. Many kinds of fossil plankton are known, but there are two groups which outdo all others in abundance and diversity. They are the *foraminifera* and the *radiolaria*, and both have a history traceable back into the Cambrian. Some of the other groups also have left fossils behind them, but we are not sure what the little creatures themselves looked like.

Fossil zooplankton is important to the geologist because of its widespread distribution, and its evolution throughout geological time helps to correlate the rocks in which they occur. Even tiny rock samples may yield large numbers of such little fossils for identification under the microscope. When the study of the sediments of the deep ocean basins began in the last century two sediments containing zooplankton skeletons were soon found to be very common. They were dubbed 'globigerina ooze' and 'siliceous ooze'. 'Globigerina ooze' includes almost all the sediments rich in calcium carbonate which are composed of coccoliths and the tests of foraminifera, especially *Globigerina*. 'Siliceous ooze' includes fine sediments with diatom cases or radiolarian tests. All these materials occur at depths down to 3500 m. At depths below 4500 m calcium carbonate seems to be dissolved and calcareous remains do not survive long. The deepest sea sediments therefore do not include such traces of the plankton from above.

Radiolarians deposit siliceous tests, collecting the silica in solution in the ocean waters. Their livelihood is dependent upon the abundance of nutrient salts and dissolved silica, and these materials are of somewhat limited distribution. Siliceous sediments are found mainly in high latitudes and also in the equatorial parts of the Pacific. As fossils, radiolaria occur mainly in siliceous rocks such as cherts.

Foraminifera. The foraminifera are a large and diverse group. Each animal is a single cell, rather irregular in shape and with slender thread-like extensions. Most of the protoplasm of the cell lies inside the test or skeleton but some extends through the many tiny openings or *foramina* of the test. They inhabit a wide range of habitats and many of them are benthonic rather than planktonic. Most are marine. Despite their small size and apparently lowly status on the tree of life, they have remarkably complex life histories.

From this basic pattern foraminifera have evolved a tremendous array of different shapes and styles. The shape, structure and composition of the test seem to be partly related to the mode of life of the animal.

The tests may be composed either of chitin or of sand, shell and other particles glued together, or of calcite. The microscopic size, shape and number of chambers present may vary from species to species. There may be one or more openings such as the *aperture* and *pores,* and there may be various kinds of surface ornamentation. The characteristics of the group are illustrated on Plate 1.

Most of the foraminifera seem to be choosy as to their environment, especially as to conditions of salinity, temperature and the nature of the sea floor. A few brackish water species are known but none occur in fresh water. Calcareous foraminifera are by far the most common in the geological record and they seem to have preferred the warmer ocean waters, as do their descendants. The largest modern foraminifera, with diameters of up to 20 mm, inhabit the tropics. Tests made of sand grains, etc. are more common in cold waters.

Today's foraminifera show a close agreement between kind and temperature or depth. Cainozoic faunas which contain many species akin to those of today can be compared closely with modern faunas, and a reasonable guess can be made of the temperature and depth at which they lived.

Planktonic foraminifera have larger and more globose tests than the benthonic kind. *Globigerina* is a typical example. Many limestones and clays from the geological column are rich in planktonic foraminifera, the tiny skeletons of which were probably produced in the sunlit layers of the sea. The earliest undoubted planktonic foraminifera are of Jurassic age. Prior to the mid-Mesozoic era these creatures may have lacked skeletons or may have lived on the bottom.

PELAGIC MOLLUSCA

Free-swimming and active members of the mollusc phylum have long been conspicuous in the fauna of the sea. Perhaps even in the Cambrian oceans they occurred locally in schools and swarms. Today two im-

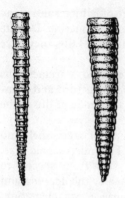

Pteropod shells are found in great numbers in some oceans today. Fossil pteropods are difficult to recognise but some of the tiny (1 cm long) shells found in the Palaeozoic rocks in countless thousands may be pteropods.

portant pelagic groups of molluscs are the *pteropods* and the *cephalopods* ('wing-foots' and 'head-foots').

Pteropods are small animals, a few centimetres long, some of which have tube-like or cone-like shells of aragonite. Most living species of pteropod inhabit the upper layers of the tropical seas. Others live in the colder waters of the oceanic depths. A small part of the Atlantic ocean floor receives a slow rain of their skeletons to make up an organic ooze.

Some of the *cephalopods* have become most successful pelagic animals and seem to have adopted this mode of life as early as the Cambrian period. Their shells are common fossils, especially in the Mesozoic rocks. Today's cephalopods include the pearly nautilus and squids, which are active nekton, and the octopus which is a benthonic and shell-less animal. All are predators, and most live in shallow water, but some species are adapted to life in the deeper zones. It was probably much the same with extinct cephalopods.

The nautilus is perhaps the closest in structure to most of the fossil cephalopods. It is a compact animal with a head bearing tentacles arranged around the mouth. The eyes are large and there is a well-developed nervous system and a circulatory system. Between the head and the lower margin of the body is a tube leading to a large cavity containing two pairs of gills. The outer body wall or mantle secretes the shell, as in other molluscs, and because the lower and side parts of the mantle do this more rapidly than the top, the shell develops into a coil. So the soft parts are encased in a calcareous tube rather like an ice-cream cone that becomes coiled up. As the animal grows the cone grows too, and at the back of the animal a partition or septum is built across the shell. Where the septum joins the outer wall a distinctive line or *suture* is produced. Periodically the animal shifts forward in the shell and a new septum has to be produced. Successive shifts produce a series of septa with hollow chambers between. Connecting the chambers to the animal is a slender tube, the *siphuncle*. There may be a short calcareous collar or *neck* on the hind side of each septum where it is perforated by the siphuncle. Some species have the septal necks connected by *connecting rings*. The chambers are filled with gas to control the creature's buoyancy, and swimming is accomplished by expelling water from the funnel to give a sort of jet-propulsion. The only real disadvantage of this means of movement seems to be that it is backwards.

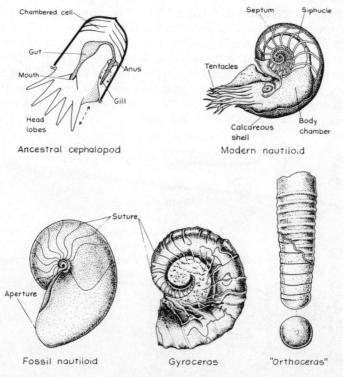

Ancestral cephalopod

Modern nautiloid

Fossil nautiloid   Gyroceras   "Orthoceras"

Cephalopods have a good fossil record and most were rather like the modern pearly nautilus, a few centimetres in diameter and possessing either an enclosing conch or a tiny internal shell like the cuttlefish. Many Palaeozoic cephalopods had straight or only slightly curved shells. (See Fig. overleaf).

The earliest undoubted cephalopods had a small straight shell with closely spaced septa. Ordovician cephalopods had straight or curved shells, some with thick connecting rings and crowded septa. Many achieved a large size – as much as 3 or 4 metres long. The *living chamber* occupies most of the shell in some forms but in others it is only a small part of the total length. Most of the straight or gently curved types may have been rather clumsy animals and all were extinct by the end of Palaeozoic time. Some of these may have been benthonic.

The completely coiled cephalopod has survived from Ordovician time to the present day. With simple suture lines, perhaps gently flexed or curved, and a relatively smooth and unornamented shell, this kind is distinguished as a *nautiloid*. All have the siphuncle on the lower or ventral side.

In Devonian cephalopod faunas, however, a tendency towards curved suture lines and less ventral siphuncles is noted. The suture lines are thrown into curves towards (*saddles*) and away from (*lobes*) the open end of the shell. *Goniatite* cephalopods (see upper fig. p. 75) evolved rapidly in late Palaeozoic times but were extinct by the end of that era.

They seem to have left descendants, however, in the *ceratite* cephalopods of the Triassic period. These are distinguished by secondary lobes and saddles on the original lobes.

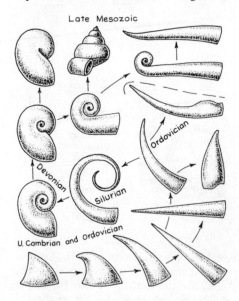

Late Mesozoic

Ordovician

Devonian

Silurian

U. Cambrian and Ordovician

Some of the many shapes taken by the nautiloids during their long and eventful history.

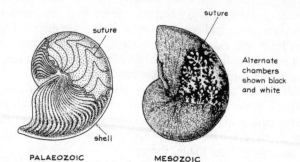

PALAEOZOIC   MESOZOIC

The Palaeozoic goniatites, ancestors of the ammonites had shells in which the septa met the outside wall along a simple zig-zag line but the true ammonites (*right*) had a much more complicated suture line.

The most conspicuous of the Jurassic and Cretaceous cephalopods are the (in most cases) coiled *ammonites*. In these the suture lines had most complicated patterns with several generations of lobes and saddles. Despite the apparently basic requirement of a coiled shell,

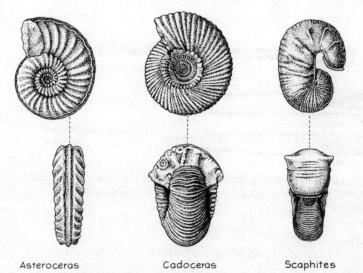

Asteroceras   Cadoceras   Scaphites

Three common British Mesozoic ammonites: *Asteroceras* from the Lower Jurassic rocks, *Cadoceras* from the Middle Jurassic, and *Scaphites* from the Cretaceous. (Approx. half natural size; from *British Mesozoic Fossils*).

some Mesozoic ammonites had loosely coiled or even straight shells. Some were globose in cross-section, others were thin and flat. The outer shell may have had corrugations and ribs, or nodes and spine-like growths, keels and ridges on the outer side. Most ammonites were a few centimetres in diameter, the largest being about 2 m across.

There is one more group of cephalopods to be included here, the *belemnoids*. These had an internal skeleton of calcium carbonate with a cone (the *phragmocone*), which was relatively small and insignificant. At the rear end of the phragmocone concentric laminae of calcite were built up to make a heavy bullet-shaped *rostrum*, while at the anterior end of the cone a long blade, the *pro-ostracum*, was formed. Only the rostrum has survived in most belemnite fossils, but the complete shells of a few species are known, and traces of even the soft anatomy are preserved in the finer clays or shales. Some Mesozoic rocks contain immense numbers of ammonites and belemnite cephalopods, and the same species have been found spread over very large areas of the world. This is some indication of how widely the cephalopods were able to travel by floating and swimming.

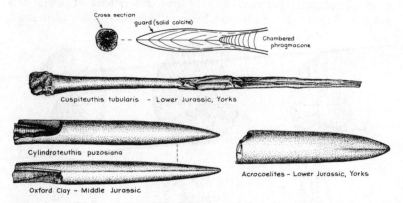

Cross section
guard (solid calcite)
Chambered phragmacone

Cuspiteuthis tubularis – Lower Jurassic, Yorks

Cylindroteuthis puzosiana

Acrocoelites – Lower Jurassic, Yorks

Oxford Clay – Middle Jurassic

Belemnites are found in marine Jurassic and Cretaceous rocks and are the internal skeletons of cuttlefish or squid-like cephalopods. These are about half-size.

THE MYSTERIOUS CONODONTS

Yet another group of animals seems to have been present in the pelagic communities of the Palaeozoic era – the conodonts. Whether they were worms, or primitive vertebrates, or of a completely different phylum

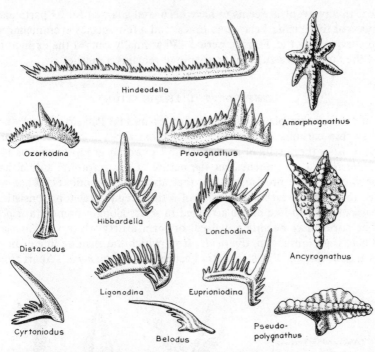

Hindeodella

Amorphognathus

Ozarkodina

Pravognathus

Distacodus

Hibbardella

Lonchodina

Ancyrognathus

Cyrtoniodus

Ligonodina

Euprioniodina

Belodus

Pseudo-
polygnathus

Some of the delicate shapes taken up by Palaeozoic conodonts. The tooth-like nature is apparent. Enlarged about 30 times.

we do not know. They are represented by microscopic phosphatic fossils that more or less resemble delicate fang-like teeth. Some rocks yield them in enormous numbers, and even allowing for the fact that any one conodont animal may have possessed many pairs of conodont 'teeth', their abundance is extraordinary. It must be admitted that no one is completely certain that they were true teeth; more probably conodonts are part of some special apparatus for grasping food rather than cutting or stabbing it. And their chemical composition is by no means a guarantee that they are related to the vertebrates.

Conodont assemblages have been found in which several different kinds occur together; but only recently was any trace of the shape of the animal itself discovered. It seems to be much as was expected – a tiny worm-like creature with a set of conodont 'teeth' at one end of the alimentary tract. Possibly it fed on plankton in the upper layers of the sea. In any event, it seems to have been well adapted for its particular mode of life during Palaeozoic times, and a few species even managed to survive into the Triassic period. What finally caused the extinction of the long-successful conodont animal remains a puzzle.

THE GRAPTOLITE QUESTION

On the bedding planes of many early or middle Palaeozoic rocks are very thin carbonaceous streaks, resembling a pencil mark. These are *graptolites,* the fossils of an extinct and puzzling group known as the *Graptolithina.* Argument over the nature of the graptolite animal has been even more prolonged than that about the conodonts. What we see today is the carbonized trace of a tiny fragile skeleton, consisting basically of cup-like *thecae* arranged in series along a branch (a *stipe*). The stipes may be single, paired, or form a network (a *rhabdosome*). There is an initial cup, the *sicula,* from which the ensuing line or lines of thecae sprang. The sicula also bears a thread (the *nema*). Apart from

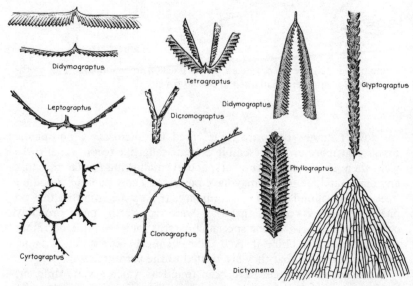

Graptolites were small colonial animals which produced skeletons of chitinous material. The general form of these elongate colonies with the individual zooids arranged in lines of thecae is about natural size. (After *British Palaeozoic Fossils*).

distinguishing differences in the shapes of the stipes and thecae, palaeontologists were for many years unable to make out very much more than this in the anatomy of the graptolites. Despite their great abundance in some rocks, they seemed invariably to have been compressed beyond further recognition. Since the 1930s graptolites have also been obtained by dissolving limestones in acids which do not harm the fossils. Some remarkable undistorted graptolites have been recovered in this way.

The graptolite fossils found by this method seem to offer more problems than we had concerning them before. The earliest graptolites are many-branched complicated rhabdosomes, the later graptolites are much simpler in construction. Moreover, the details of graptolite anatomy suggest that these early forms, the late Cambrian *dendroid* graptolites, had three distinct kinds of thecae. Each theca housed a little individual animal or *zooid*, and in the colony an individual zooid gave rise to three new zooids, one of which was like its predecessor and occupied the axis of the stipe. The other two zooids produced thecae which opened laterally from the stipe and were in detail different from one another. No doubt each kind of zooid had a special function in the colony, food catching, protection, respiration or reproduction. They are connected internally by a tiny tube or *stolon*. All the thecal walls are delicately constructed of thin strings or sheets of material.

Later graptolites had only one kind of theca and lacked stolons, seeming more primitive than the dendroid forms. The number of stipes was reduced in the Ordovician and Silurian periods until the last graptolites had only one.

What manner of creature was the graptolite? Marine, colonial, planktonic or pelagic, it certainly was, but what relatives it has in today's zoological catalogue is not so certain. Graptolites have been regarded as sponges, simple coelenterates, bryozoa and pterobranchs. Perhaps they are in some respects more like the coelenterates than other groups, but the similarity is not really very striking. On the other hand, the stolon that connects the thecae and the composition of the skeleton resemble those of pterobranchs. Pterobranchs are small, colonial, filter feeding, sessile benthonic creatures with chitinous skeletons. Some zoologists regard them as rather interesting relatives of the chordate phylum, but the similarities are not obvious.

In mode of life graptolites must have been planktonic, some apparently had a bladder-like float attached to the nema. Others may have been anchored to seaweeds. Together they may have drifted over immense distances – the same species being found in North America,

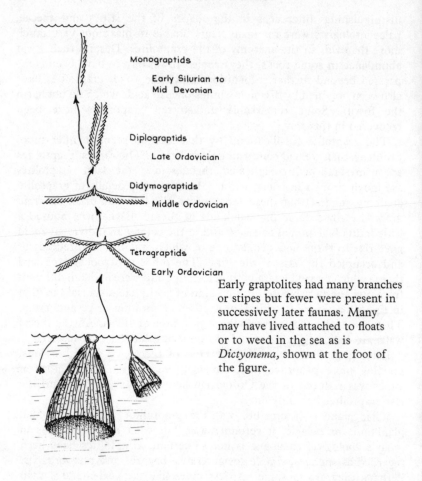

Monograptids

Early Silurian to
Mid Devonian

Diplograptids

Late Ordovician

Didymograptids

Middle Ordovician

Tetragraptids

Early Ordovician

Early graptolites had many branches
or stipes but fewer were present in
successively later faunas. Many
may have lived attached to floats
or to weed in the sea as is
Dictyonema, shown at the foot of
the figure.

Europe and Australia, for example. One may imagine that, like many
planktonic organisms today, they rose and descended through the
upper layers of the sea in response to light or temperature or feeding
conditions. The cilia, or tentacles or other protrusible parts of the
zooids, would perhaps guide or assist this movement and ensure the
passage of plankton and food particles to the right parts of the colony.

Most graptolite enthusiasts have pictured the colonies floating with
the thecae opening upwards, but it has been argued that perhaps such
a view is upside down. The rhabdosomes would have been in life
orientated with the thecae opening downwards with the activity of

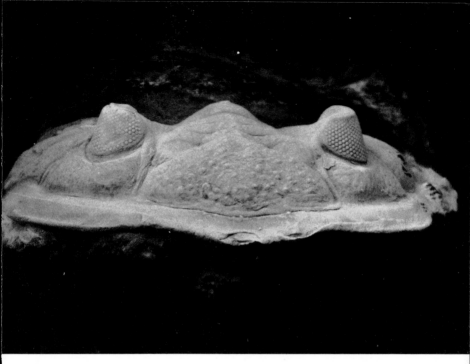

PLATE 5. Amongst the most intensely studied but still puzzling fossils are the segmented marine trilobites. Here are two views of the head shield of *Dalmanites* (× 2), a form with many faceted eyes like a fly. The mouth was on the under surface of the head: *above*, from in front; *below*, from above.

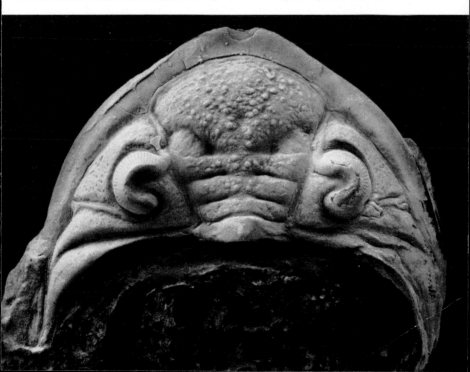

PLATE 6. A blind trilobite, *Conocoryphe* (× 3.5), clearly different from *Dalmanites* in having no eyes, shows the characteristic tri-lobed head, body segments and tail. Legs, antennae etc. are not preserved but were present underneath this carapace.

the zooids forming a current that pushed the colony upwards through the water. When the zooids were at rest the rhabdosome slowly sank. Some forms may have had a spiral cr helical course, but alas, all this is speculation. The graptolites died out in Devonian time, perhaps gobbled up by successful marine predators. Early in Devonian time there were certainly plenty of likely predators, conspicuous being the fish. The graptolites may have been plankton sweepers, but by the end of the early Devonian they had themselves been swept away. Only their puzzling skeletons remain for us to argue about.

PETROLIFEROUS POSTSCRIPT

This quick look at plankton and possible members of the ancient planktonic community suggests that there has, since the earliest times, been an enormous wealth of tiny living things floating in the seas. Very probably a food chain based on plankton has existed in one form or another since Precambrian time. The phytoplankton has not only formed the first link in this chain, it has spread sheets of chalky sediment across the sea floors. The zooplankton too has contributed to the deposition of calcareous and siliceous sediments by the rain of tiny skeletons. But the soft tissues of the plankton may have added very substantially to the quantities of soft organic matter being incorporated in the marine sediments. As the sediments were converted to rock, the dead organic components have been transformed, distilled and condensed into a complex assembly of new organic materials, hydrocarbons.. With pressure, heat and time, petroleum may have been generated from the organic debris buried beneath the sea floor. The plankton relied upon solar energy to power its life processes and organize its biochemicals. In the lithosphere these biochemicals have been reorganized and altered in a chain of changes that has resulted in crude oil and natural gas. Under the right geological conditions these substances accumulate locally in the pores and fissures of the rock. Oil and gas fields are the result. Burning this oil, we unleash the energy that reached the earth millions of years ago. Like coal, petroleum has been called a fossil fuel – a product of organisms long since dead. Many a limestone has, when freshly broken, an oily smell, the product perhaps of chemical changes begun long ago in the plankton-rich waters of an ancient sea.

CHAPTER 4

BENTHOS: LIFE AT THE BOTTOM

BY late Precambrian time (see p. 21) living things had begun new ways of utilizing and colonizing marine environments. The advantages of a planktonic vagrant existence were many, but other ways of life had their attractions. With a constant rain of corpses and organic matter falling to the sea floor there was plenty of opportunity for scavengers and carrion feeders there, for the sluggish and the sedentary. Even during the earliest phases of evolution there must have been organisms dependent upon this food supply, and the benthonic community was probably a large one. Today it is still dominated by microscopic bacteria, diatoms, some fungi and the algal plants (seaweed). While some of these must have sunlight, others manage just as well in the dark. Feeding on them in turn is a substantial variety of simple animals, many of which do not need sunlight and range from the shoreline down to the lightless depths of the oceans. Late Precambrian fossils include widespread and varied benthonic types. They were undoubtedly flourishing in many of the shallow waters near or along coastlines. Since Precambrian times the benthonic part of the biosphere has been most prolific, and the most common fossils are those of the marine benthos.

There are two reasons why bottom-dwelling sea life has left us such a good record. One is that many animals have acquired shells or other hard parts that resist decomposition when the animal dies; the other is that into the coastal waters there is a constant flow of sediment from the land. The shells and other animal debris were quickly buried by mud or sand and soon were fossilized. Nevertheless the first benthonic animal groups of which we have any trace are without hard parts. From several places, South Australia in particular, we have surprisingly well-preserved impressions of soft-bodied creatures. Some of them are peculiar forms, unlike animals living now, which were perhaps left stranded on the mud by some Precambrian high tide. Such early fossils are, however, very rare, and not until animal life had evolved to construct shells and skeletons was there much to be included in the record. In early Cambrian times natural selection had produced hard tissues in several types of sea creatures, but it was not until the Ordovician

TABLE OF HABITATS

		Filter-Feeders	Sediment-Feeders	Herbivores	Carnivores and Scavengers
EPIFAUNAL (living on the surface of the sea floor)	Mobile	Crustacea		Snails Sea Urchins	Snails Worms Crustacea Star fishes Brittle Stars
	Attached	Sponges Bryozoa Brachiopoda Clams Crustacea Crinoidea			Corals Sea anemones
INFAUNAL (living buried in the sea floor)	Burrowing in soft sediment	Clams	Clams Worms	Clams Worms Brittle Stars Sea Urchins	Snails Crustacea
	Boring in Hard Rock or Wood	Sponges Clams			

Benthonic animals may be epifaunal or infaunal, but many other creatures may temporarily be either at some stage of their existence.

period, twenty-five million years after the Cambrian, that a calcareous house or suit of armour first came generally into fashion.

HOW TO SUCCEED ON THE BOTTOM

The prime demand of any organism is a good supply of food. It has been the controlling factor in the development of all animal communities. The regular square meal makes the difference between success and mere survival or extinction. Animals in the sea have evolved very successful ways of getting their food, as we saw with the pelagic groups. It is worth noting at the outset that the benthonic modes of life centre upon the essential task of getting food. Protection from other animals (in search of *their* food) and reproduction come second. We can easily distinguish in the benthonic animals four common ways of feeding:

1. the *herbivores* graze or feed on benthonic algae,
2. the *carnivores* and scavengers devour other animals, living or dead,
3. the *filter-feeders* strain plankton from the water and food particles from the sea-floor waters,

4. the *sediment-feeders* gulp in mud or sand and extract food from it as it passes through the gut.

Over many parts of the sea floor there are as many, if not more, animals living buried in the bottom sediment (*infaunas*) as resting or moving on top of it (*epifaunas*). Some sixteen combinations of feeding and infaunal or epifaunal habit are possible and some animal groups have successfully adapted to more than one habitat. Snails, clams, worms and crustaceans are among the versatile; other types such as corals, bryozoa, brachiopods and crinoids have stuck in the mud or to one habitat only.

Those that in Cambrian times evolved successfully for feeding in one or other of the benthonic habitats produced other protective devices and aids to living. Shells and skeletons, usually worn on the outside, were the most efficient. Different phyla of animals have produced hard parts, fashioned in carbonate in most cases. This activity has been important in the evolution of life itself in the sea but has had a marked geological effect in the accumulation of shelly and other limestones.

Shells and heavy hard parts are rather a hindrance to wandering about the sea floor. Most of the animals possessing them are slow movers or burrowers or are firmly anchored so as not to move at all. A *sessile* (or sitting) mode of life has claimed many groups, and they manage to hold their own without ever leaving their chosen sites. Their distribution over the sea floor is achieved by eggs or larvae drifting about before settling on a suitable site. Most of the sessile benthos reproduce by liberating countless reproductive cells into the sea, the male and female depending on chance meeting for fusion. The fertilized cells drift around, most being gobbled up by other animals, until only a few survive into a larval stage. The larvae may be planktonic or free swimming before metamorphosing into sessile adults. Does this indicate that the sessile animals have evolved from early vagrant forms? Not necessarily, but probably, and it is worth noting that no hard parts are formed until this metamorphosis begins.

Of course many of the vagrant benthos have shells and similarly pass through metamorphoses from egg to larva and adult. All of them have the same enormous reproductive capacity as the sessile animals. Even when the individuals reach maturity the competition for living space and food continues.

It is rarely, if ever, the case that a habitat is occupied by only one kind of animal. Usually there is a wide variety of species, animals of different phyla all existing together in communities, benthonic or not. The coral reef, for example, is a habitat made up primarily of coral polyps and dead coral skeletons, but it offers a home and happy hunting-ground for an extremely large number of other creatures, from protozoa to sharks.

Different species may live side by side without harming one another, but there is always a limit to the number of individuals of any species that a habitat can support. Some communities on the sea floor are of well-spaced-out individuals, others are crowded. Distribution depends on many factors, but the availability of food is the most important. Many a bed of fossiliferous rock, the deposit of an ancient sea floor, shows that the same was true in past eras.

PROTOZOA

While many protozoa are planktonic and others benthonic, neither kind is likely to leave fossil remains unless it has hard parts. The foraminifera are represented by benthonic types as well as planktonic forms. Both the calcareous and the arenaceous foraminifera are present in the benthos and locally in Palaeozoic rocks they may be enormously abundant. As we saw in Chapter 3, the foraminifera are very fussy about their environment, but we know less about the preferences of the foraminifera of the past. Having given these fossils a good share of the limelight in the preceding chapter, we may pass on to the larger animals, the metazoa, with their layers of uniform cells.

PORIFERA

The porifera, or sponges, are the simplest metazoa and most of them dwell in salty water. In appearance they are like blobs or bottles of dark jelly, and rare specimens grow as big as 1 m across.

Sponge anatomy is very simple, and although they are metazoa, sponges have only three different types of cell. There are cells to cover the outside surface, cells with flagellae to line the inner canals and surfaces, and amoeboid cells here and there in the gelatinous substance between the canals. The flagellate cells waft water through the system and extract food particles from it. The amoeboid cells help distribute the food. Apart from this, each cell functions as a self-contained unit. The individual sponge thus resembles a colony of flagellate protozoa, but there is in sponges a skeleton composed either of microscopic rods (*spicules*) of silica or calcite, or of tough fibres of *spongin*. Sponges like

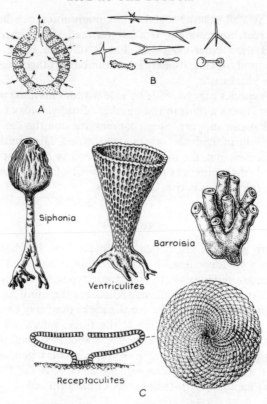

Sponges feed by filtering food from currents of water set up in their sack-like bodies (A). Their skeletons are composed of innumerable tiny spicules of silica or lime (B) and take on many shapes (C). *Receptaculites* looks like a flat sponge but may be a completely different kind of organism. Nothing like it exists today. (All about quarter size).

clear water and dislike mud – it clogs their system. In the past, as today, sponges spread in large numbers over coral reef seas.

Probably the sponges evolved in Precambrian times from flagellate protozoans, over which they represent a great advance in organization. Once their pattern of life was established, however, these 'unambitious' animals seem never to have evolved much from the pattern set up long ago. When a sponge dies the spicules are soon scattered and so complete fossil sponges are rather rare. Nevertheless they do occur in great numbers in some rocks.

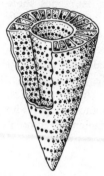   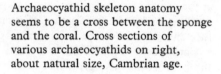 

Archaeocyathid skeleton anatomy seems to be a cross between the sponge and the coral. Cross sections of various archaeocyathids on right, about natural size, Cambrian age.

Some not very common Palaeozoic fossils may be close relatives of sponges. In these regular plate-like spicules build up hollow flat or bun-shaped structures rather like sunflower heads.

ARCHAEOCYATHA

Although not common in Europe, the archaeocyatha deserve mention because they may be a 'missing link' between the porifera and the corals. They occur in early and middle Cambrian rocks, i.e. later than the first sponges and before the stony corals.

Each archaeocyathid is basically two vertical cones or tubes of carbonate, one inside the other, and up to 15 cm long. The cones are connected by many vertical plates or septa arranged radially, and the whole is perforated by small pores. One can imagine that this anatomy allowed water to circulate to all parts of the animal as in the sponges, yet the cone-like construction with its apparent symmetry is very like a Palaeozoic coral. Some forms branched and made colonies, others grew singly. Mounds and banks of archaeocyathid skeletons on the sea floor provided shelter for whole benthonic communities, and when the Ordovician and later coral-like animals gave rise to reefs, the benthos were ready to take similar advantage.

COELENTERATA

Of the several kinds of coelenterates in the seas today only the stony corals have much fossil record. Fossil jellyfish or sea anemones are very rare, but from Ordovician time onwards the benthos includes corals of one kind or another. While the jellyfish represent one line of evolution of the coelenterates, the corals and sea anemones show another. The basic unit in these little animals is the polyp – a simple blind sac, bag or stomach with tentacles arranged around the mouth at the top. There is a primitive nervous system, and reproduction is by budding or by the production of germ cells liberated into the sea to fuse and grow into new individuals. It is a simple life.

Coral polyps may be more sophisticated, but their simple relatives, the hydrozoans, also grow in colonies of many thousand polyps. The puzzling *stromatoporoids* may be the calcareous remains of colonial

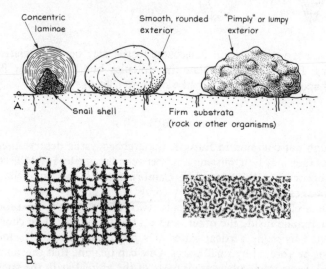

Stromatoporoids (A) are cabbage-shaped or rounded masses of very thin calcium carbonate layers. Some began by attaching to a coral, snail or other shell, later smothering it. Large colonies reach a metre or more across and formed reefs and mounds on the sea floor. Their microstructure (B) is used in identification, but the animal which produced it remains unknown.

hydrozoa. They are bun-shaped masses of thin concentric lamellae, rather like stalagmite. Each layer has a microscopic structure with tiny cavities and solid pillars. These may have served as a foundation for a hydrozoan colony, new layers being added as the colony grew. Stromatoporoids are found grown around a snail or other object that lay on the sea floor. They first appeared in Ordovician time, but by the mid Silurian they throve even to the extent of building great mound-like reefs, a habit they shared with the corals. Some of these reefs may be seen in the old quarries on Wenlock Edge, at Wren's Nest, Dudley, and in Devonian rocks at Torquay. In Mesozoic and later reefs they are replaced by the *millepores*.

The essential piece of coral hardware is a cup or base in which the polyp resides. As the animal grows, new calcium carbonate is added. To improve its feeding efficiency the polyp wall has a regular number of infolds supported by vertical plate-like septa arranged radially within the cup. These afford the polyp a greater surface area for feeding and a better grasp on its cup. There may be further calcareous structures to support the animal as it grows. Horizontal plates (tabulae, tabellae), axial rods or meshworks (*columellae*) and marginal plates linking the septa (*dissepiments*) all help in this task.

Corals can multiply by budding or by sexual reproduction, so the polyps may exist singly or have a colonial habit where the many polyp-holding cups (*corallites*) are united into a single mass (*corallum*). Most reef-building corals are of the colonial kind.

On the basis of the shape and symmetrical arrangement of the internal plates within the corallites, three different groups of fossil corals are recognized:

1. *Tetracorals* or *Rugosa* (Palaeozoic). A conical calcareous corallite with a general four-fold (biradial) symmetry and in some forms axial rods and marginal structures as well as septa.
2. *Hexacorals* (Mesozoic-Recent). Like the rugosa but with a wide variety of form and a six-fold symmetry.
3. *Tabulata* (Palaeozoic). Colonial corals with many individual tubes, fused or connected by tubules and with many horizontal tabulae. The septa are rudimentary or absent.

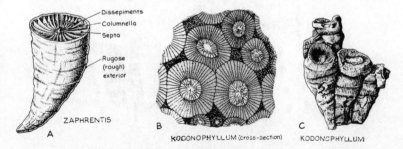

The rugose or horn corals of the Palaeozoic era lived as isolated individuals (as in A) or clustered and fused together (as in B and C). Their skeletal parts were relatively simple. (About natural size).

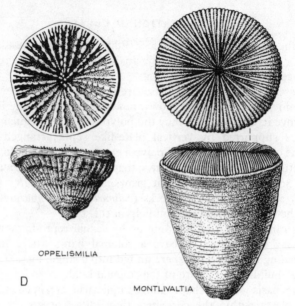

OPPELISMILIA

D

MONTLIVALTIA

Two common British Jurassic hexacorals. (About natural size).

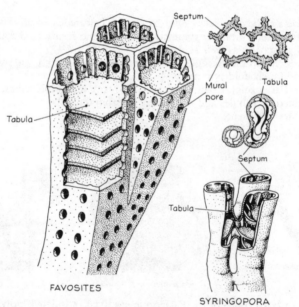

Septum

Mural pore

Tabula

Tabula

Septum

Tabula

Tabula

FAVOSITES

SYRINGOPORA

The tabulate corals are so-called because of the many tiny tabulae that underlay each polyp. (× 8; after Beerbower).

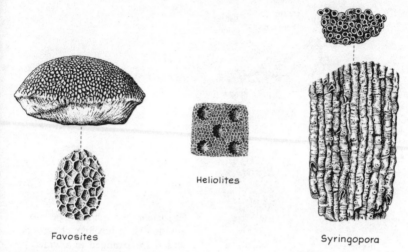

Heliolites

Favosites   Syringopora

Some typical tabulates from British formations. (About natural size; after *British Palaeozoic Fossils*).

BRYOZOA

Another phylum of animals that early adopted a colonial mode of life in the sea, the bryozoa, is puzzling in many respects, and we know little or nothing of its origin. Each individual in the colony is tiny, but the colony may·consist of many thousands of individuals and have the appearance of fronds of moss (the name *bryozoa* means moss-animal), twigs or mould-like encrustations. Each little animal constructs a calcareous cup or box (*zooecium*) and from this protrude tiny tentacles to catch food. Within the cup are muscles which can pull in the soft parts when danger is at hand. Although there is a gut and a separate anus, the bryozoa lack specialized circulatory, respiratory or excretory systems. Clearly they are more highly organized than the coelenterates. They have a free-swimming larval stage, and once a larva has settled a new individual springs up and begins to breed until eventually a large colony is formed.

See next page for fig.

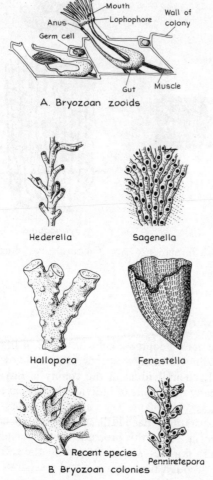

A. Bryozoan zooids

Bryozoan apartments. The tiny zooids live in box-like chambers which are arranged in a wide variety of ways, in fronds, flat sheets, etc. (Fossil species about natural size; after Beerbower).

B. Bryozoan colonies

BRACHIOPODA

Brachiopods crowded the Palaeozoic benthos and seem to have 'sought' the company of the corals and bryozoa in particular. The brachiopod star diminished with the rise of the shelly molluscs in the Mesozoic, and today the group is no longer much in evidence. Most brachiopods are housed in two small shells or valves of calcium carbonate: less numerous are those brachiopods which have chitinophosphatic shells. Although neither seem at first glance to have much in common with the colonial bryozoa, they have rather the same general plan as the bryozoa in their structure. They were sessile but not colonial and each individual was much larger than the bryozoan zooid, or even than entire bryozoa colonies.

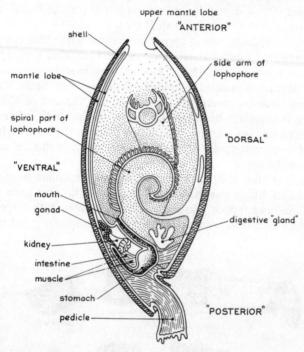

Brachiopod anatomy. Between the two shells or valves lay the brachiopod's soft parts. The pedicle was attached to a firm hold such as a rock – or another brachiopod, but many fossil brachiopods seem to have dispensed with their pedicles in later life.

Firmly anchored to the bottom as most brachiopods were, they evolved patterns of folds at the edges of their shells to admit plenty of water but exclude sand, mud and predators. Much of the available space inside the shells is taken up by a coiled filter-feeding device, the lophophore. On the arms of this are tiny hair-like cilia which waft along currents of water and pass food to the mouth. In most brachiopods there is a calcareous support for the lophophore, and in many ancient species it was a pair of delicate spines or coils filling much of the interior.

Brachiopods may fix themselves to the substrate by a long fleshy 'stem', the pedicle, and there are groups that lie free on the bottom or cement one valve to something solid. Many extinct brachiopods had spines which may have kept them in place on the sea floor. Other adaptations for successful feeding and survival included drastic modifications of the brachiopod shell form.

First of the brachiopods to appear were those with chitinous valves, the Inarticulata. They arrived early in the Cambrian period. Their shells lacked the well-designed hinge of later brachiopods, but they had several pairs of muscles to hold the shells together. Some (*Lingula*) had a long pedicle; others were cemented. By the end of Cambrian times the inarticulate brachiopods reached their zenith, after which they have never been so numerous. Their place in the benthos became more and more restricted as the articulate brachiopods and the molluscs came upon the scene.

Equipped with hinged calcareous shells, the Articulata were new in the Cambrian, but it was in the Ordovician that the first great spread of articulate brachiopods occurred. It corresponded with a spread of shallow seas over land areas and with a general increase in all manner

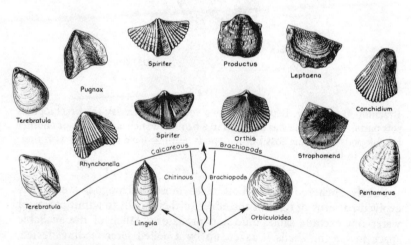

Fossil brachiopods are common and important members of the ancient benthos. By far the most common are the calcareous shelled forms, but most are now extinct. Not all to same scale.

of marine life. The heyday of the brachiopods was in late Silurian and early Devonian time, since when they have been dwindling. Although they managed to put up a brave show till the end of the Palaeozoic era they were not tenacious enough to enter more than two orders of Articulata and two of Inarticulata for the Mesozoic stakes.

Being sensitive to environmental conditions and evolving rapidly throughout the Palaeozoic era, these fossils are very useful as indices of geological time and marine habitat. Thick-shelled, large, abundant forms indicate water of little depth; thin-shelled forms lived in deeper water. *Lingula* is alive and well today, frequenting waters that are often brackish or tidal. It is the only fossil present in some rocks, and the adjacent strata may have only terrestrial or freshwater fossil plants and animals.

WORMS AND THE LIKE

So far the benthos we have dredged up have all been very simply designed animals, content to be sessile. Searching further, however, we soon met the active creepie-crawlies of various kinds. Most of them seem to be segmented. This character consists of a repetition of part of the animal several times along its axis – it is a zoologically interesting development which seems to have opened up all sorts of new avenues for evolution. Worms, arthropods and even some molluscs are segmented to a greater or lesser degree and traces of a kind of segmentation are found in higher animals too.

We do not know how this kind of construction originated, but it had provided the basis for several experiments in living before the Cambrian period. Possibly it arose in animals that had a burrowing habit and found that short chunks of muscle along their length helped in locomotion. Their primitive longitudinal muscles became bunched

Peripatus looks like a caterpillar but is in fact intermediate between worms and arthropods. It seems to be a kind of 'living fossil', representing the type of creature from which the insects first developed in early Palaeozoic time.

and grouped for a wriggling burrowing life. Other organs perhaps had to be reorganized as a result. When swimming was added to these animals' performance segmentation was not in every case a handicap. Different segments could take on different functions – as we shall see with the arthropods. One or more of the segments up in front became highly organized, and in several different groups of animals a head region must have taken on the functions it has retained ever since. Cambrian fossils show just how successful the early variations on this theme had become.

But we should return to the simplest segmented animals in the benthos. Most of them lack preservable hard parts and very few fossils show what the soft anatomy was like. Some worms possess tiny chitinous jaw elements, known as scolecodonts, which are common micro-fossils in some rocks.

Annelids (segmented worms) are busy creatures which are today among the most abundant, varied and important members of the benthos. They have explored many different habitats and adopted each of the different feeding methods. It is a pity that so few worms

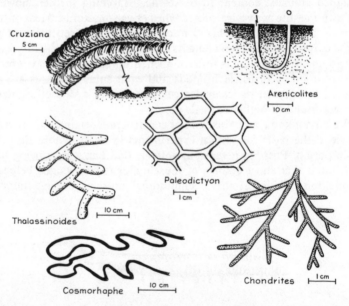

Some trace-fossils; the marks left on bedding surfaces and within sedimentary rocks which are the tracks, burrows and other signs of animal activity in the ancient environments.

PLATE 7. *Above*, Stromatolites, the layered structures produced by lime-secreting algae range in size from minute to bodies many metres in diameter. Here is a layer of carboniferous stromatolites. (Courtesy Institute of Geological Sciences, Crown Copyright reserved.) *Below*, a polished cross-section of a single colony from the Purbeck Beds of Dorset (× 1.5).

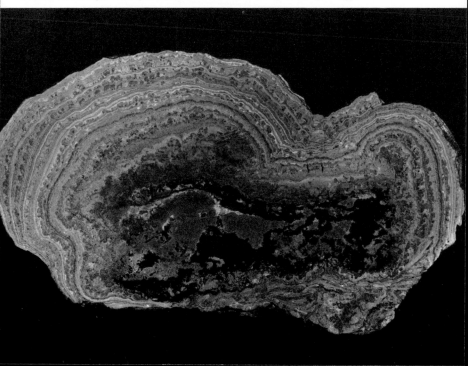

PLATE 8. *Above,* Graptolites of several different kinds are preserved on the surface of this fine black shale from the Ordovician of South Wales (× 0.5). *Below,* Conodonts in abundance surprisingly preserved as casts and moulds in a shale surface from the Lower Carboniferous of Cornwall (× 25).

became fossilized. Some modern annelids construct distinctive burrows, others secrete calcareous tubes in which to live and these do occur as fossils. More and more attention has been given recently to studying *trace fossils*, the burrows, tracks and trails. By comparing them with the products of modern animals we can infer the presence of organisms which have left no other signs of their existence.

ARTHROPODS

Whatever the success of the phyla we have discussed so far, it is nothing as compared with what the arthropods, the jointed-legged beasts, have achieved. They have invaded every environment and one group, the insects, outbids all others for pride of place among the arthropods. Arthropods have, however, not as good a geological record as we would wish. They have been too active to get caught up in many processes of fossilization.

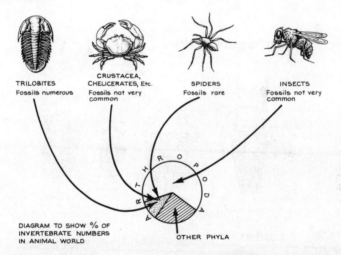

TRILOBITES
Fossils numerous

CRUSTACEA,
CHELICERATES, Etc.
Fossils not very
common

SPIDERS
Fossils rare

INSECTS
Fossils not very
common

DIAGRAM TO SHOW % OF
INVERTEBRATE NUMBERS
IN ANIMAL WORLD

OTHER PHYLA

Modern arthropods, especially insects, are very abundant, but fossil arthropods have left an uneven record. All are made of rather perishable materials.

Even in the lowest Cambrian rocks there are arthropods, well developed and diverse. The Cambrian fauna is dominated by the *trilobites*, and this group of marine arthropods was brought to extinction only at the end of Permian time by the ever-increasing competition from newer, more effective groups of arthropods. Their record survives

F.   G

largely because they added calcium carbonate to their complex
exoskeletons and they abounded in shallow seas. Some were tiny;
others up to 40 cm long; most were about 5 cm long.

Typically the trilobites were benthonic scavengers, swimming and

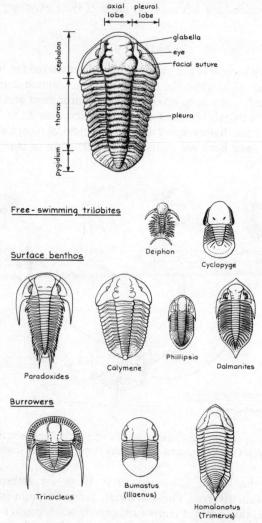

Some of the most famous of all fossils, the trilobites, were an abundant
benthos in many Palaeozoic seas. About half size or smaller.

crawling over the bottom sediments, perhaps even burrowing in the mud. Their trilobed character is apparent in the three regions, head, thorax and tail. Head and tail are made up of fused and modified segments, but the thorax is formed by a variable number of free articulating segments. The trilobite head has many variations, developed, no doubt, as adaptations for modes of life on the sea floor. The eyes in some are made up of a large number of separate lenses, like an insect's. Some eyes are raised on stalks. Sight was thus important for some trilobites, but others who may have dwelt in mud or in deep dark waters managed with poor eyesight or none at all. On the underside of the head were projecting antennae and four pairs of double legs, and the mouth. The other feature to note on the trilobite head is the pair of sutures separating the cheeks from the central part. We think trilobites shed their skeletons several times during life and that in the process the facial sutures split open and the animal crawled out.

Beneath the middle lobe of the thorax were the gut and other organs. Under the side lobes of the body and tail were more double legs, one pair per segment. These remarkable double limbs consisted of a leg-like member for walking and a gill-like member for swimming and respiration.

Many trilobites were prickly or spiny and some may have used this character as an aid to floating rather than as an essentially protective measure.

Trilobites were numerous and successful, one of the most fascinating of all fossil groups. But they were not the only arthropods in the Palaeozoic. In the Cambrian we see several other kinds of jointed-legged animals. One of them is a possible ancestor of a group, the *chelicerates*, which includes the eurypterids, spiders and scorpions. Eurypterids were truly nightmare animals, rather like scorpions in appearance, up to 2 m in length and living in estuaries and lagoons. Many were probably voracious predators. Appearing first in the Ordovician period, they reached their acme in Siluro-Devonian times and then dwindled into extinction in the Permian.

We may be grateful that the more familiar arthropods of today include no eurypterids but do include the often appetizing *crustaceans*. For the other extant arthropods such as *insects* and *myriapods* most of us have mixed feelings. While the crustaceans are very common members of the benthos, the myriapods, millipedes and centipedes are the oldest and most primitive land arthropods, and insects have buzzed in the air since Devonian times. Dragon-flies and other insects in the

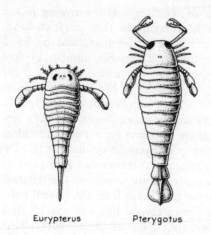

Ancient 'sea scorpions' or Eurypterids were usually a few centimetres long but the biggest over 2 m long. Their skeletons were, nevertheless, rather flimsy. (About one third life-size).

Eurypterus   Pterygotus

late Carboniferous forests were six to eight times their present size.

The *ostracoda* are a conspicuous group of small crustaceans, found in fresh and marine waters alike. Their fossils resemble tiny beans and are found in rocks of all ages from Ordovician on. Larger crustaceans, the crabs, lobsters, shrimps, prawns and barnacles, are still important members of the benthos. They have left few fossils because most of them have little calcium carbonate in their skeletons and the corpses never survived long enough for preservation. Those that did seem to be remarkably like modern forms. Geologists dismiss them as perhaps a rather conservative and uninteresting group who first appear in Cambrian rocks.

MOLLUSCS

We came across the molluscs in our look at the plankton, but now it is time to say something more about them. They really are a versatile and ubiquitous group with a history as varied as any. Despite first appearances, they have a close relationship to the annelids. Perhaps the ancient wormy stock may have given the first molluscs their start in life. The proto-mollusc was undoubtedly a benthonic crawler, moving along by ripple-like contractions of the ventral muscles. Such muscles were to become the *foot*, above it rose the *visceral hump* covered by the tough 'skin' or *mantle*. In time the mantle became the site of calcium carbonate deposition – it grew the shell, it also folded over sideways to enclose a space in which *gills* were situated. The head region may have had eyes, a pair of sensory tentacles and a mouth with a tiny protrusible toothed 'tongue' or *radula* for rasping away at food. From this kind of animal several kinds of mollusc may have evolved around the end of Precambrian times – the snails, the clams, the cephalopods, and a ragbag of other shelly creatures.

The more primitive molluscs were all small. The *monoplacophora*, possibly the nearest to an annelid, have small conical shells with paired muscle scars. The *amphineura* or chitons have a row of calcareous plates along the back and have several internal characters that may be retained from the distant past. Finally, in a group of small burrowing molluscs, the

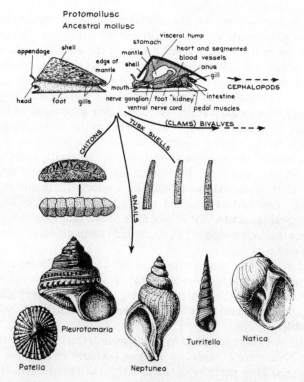

Protomollusc is a convenient name for an animal that may have been the ancestor of all the great mollusc families. Although the shells of the chitons and tusk-shells are very different their inhabitants are basically similar. Snails in coiled shells have achieved the greatest success in adapting to different ways of life. (About natural size).

Scaphopods (tusk-shells), the anatomy is condensed to occupy a cone from which the foot protrudes. None of these groups is very common among fossils.

The *gastropoda* (snails and slugs) have lost bilateral symmetry by developing a twist, though why they should do this is not understood. They have evolved gills for breathing in sea or fresh water, or lungs for life on land. Their shells have become modified (or lost) for every way of life from burrowing to swimming. On the shell surface may appear knobs, ridges, spines and coloured ornament, but the significance of these often escapes us. Although snails are locally abundant, it is perhaps surprising to see how little or (appropriately) how slowly they have evolved over the years. A contented lot, perhaps.

The *bivalvia* (clams), another familiar molluscan group, are also known as pelecypods and as lamellibranchs because of the hatchet-shape of the foot and the layered nature of the gills. Indeed, between the two shells has developed a thoroughly versatile organism, filter-feeding in most cases and crawling, burrowing, or just lying cemented or tied to the sea floor as is the wont of the various bivalve groups. By analogy with modern shells we can suggest what mode of life fossil clams had. In almost every species one shell is the mirror image of the other. Where the species creeps around the sea floor there is a pro-nounced foot which emerges from between the shells, and the shells themselves are equilateral. Burrowing clams are long and slender or narrow. Oysters and edible mussels have adopted a sessile existence, becoming cemented or attached to the floor or to rocks and other surfaces. Scallops and a few others have found that they can swim by rapid opening and closing of the shells and creating a small jet of water for propulsion.

For each of these various modes of life the musculature needed to open and close the valves evolved to equal the task imposed on it, and the two valves may articulate along a hinge line. Any clam that cannot open and close the valves or keep them securely closed at will has trouble.

The bivalvia first appeared in Ordovician waters and by the end of Silurian time were common in shallow seas and in brackish or even fresh waters. They made moderate progress until the Jurassic, but have since become widespread and dominate the larger benthos over huge areas. Large numbers of different bivalves live in the same areas and the widest variety occurs in the shallow subtropical seas today.

The *cephalopoda* are a different matter altogether and, as we saw in Chapter 3, have played a major role in the pelagic faunas of the past. They

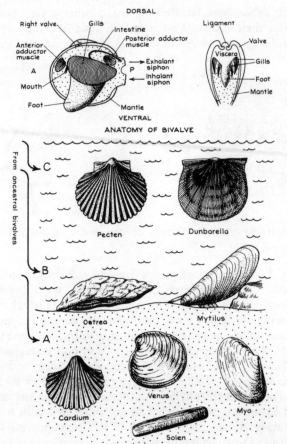

The bivalves are found in most watery environments and some are redoubtable rock builders (oysters). Many burrow in sand or mud (A), and some lie on the surface (B, *Ostrea* is an oyster) and a few are swimmers, as perhaps was the fossil *Dunbarella* (C).

are, nevertheless, on the wane today. Many, no doubt, were benthonic in habit, as is the shell-less octopus.

ECHINODERMATA

The common starfish and the prickly sea urchin are members of the echinodermata, the spiny-skinned, who in all their long history have never, as far as we know, left the salty sea for other waters. Somewhere back in time their ancestors hit upon a unique hydraulic device, the *water vascular system*, to aid locomotion, feeding and respiration. At

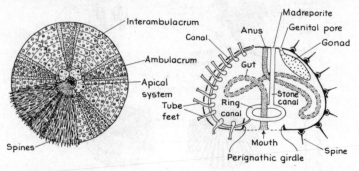

The characteristic echinoid anatomy of little plates, spines and tube feet. (About natural size).

some early stage too they adopted a five-fold radial symmetry, though several early echinoderm kinds evolved in other ways that were not successful enough to persist. The common ancestor of all these was perhaps bilaterally symmetrical, with tentacles around the mouth and a new-found ability to secrete a skeleton of calcium carbonate plates beneath the skin. Perhaps it was also sessile or only a sluggish mover, as were the early Palaeozoic types. Echinoderms seem as a group to have been exercised whether finally to move around or to stay put. On several occasions the phylum has increased its numbers and kinds, prompted by an increasing ability to get about and grab food. Four basic, and relatively successful, patterns of structure appeared by Ordovician times as shown on p. 105.

The earliest echinodermata appear in the Cambrian rocks, but are rare indeed and need not detain us here. The *edrioasteroids*, however, are worth a glance. Small bun-shaped or discoidal sacs made of tiny plates, they have on their upper surfaces five curving rays (ambulacra) of paired plates. Within the rays are minute pores and at the centre of the surface is a larger hole. These pores must be for part of the water vascular system where it extended beneath the ray and sent out tiny, paired, water-inflated podia to catch food and to pass it along to the mouth. Edrioasteroids were firmly cemented to a shell or other smooth surface. They must have had planktonic larvae as have modern echinoderms, but in Carboniferous times they became extinct.

The sac-like *cystoids* were more common and were endowed with a

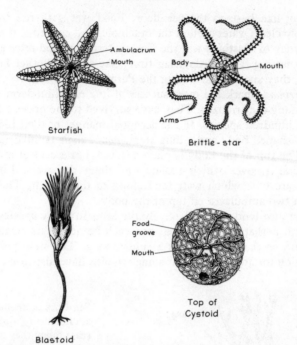

Other members of the echinodermata: the blastoids and cystoids lived only in Palaeozoic times (About half size).

skeleton of numerous, somewhat irregular, plates. At the top and centre was the mouth, with up to five ambulacra radiating from it to the short arms (brachioles). The arms and the plate (*madreporite*) by which water entered the vascular system are also on the upper surface. Some cystoids had long stems, others short; a stemless few may have been free. Over the surface of the cystoid sac is a distinctive and puzzling pattern of pores which modern echinoderms lack. Perhaps the pores aided respiration or other metabolic processes.

The *blastoids* seem to be an attempt to achieve by more regular symmetry and economy of structure all that the cystoids did. They are also larger and more common than were the cystoids. Notice how the ambulacra are large and conspicuous and the number of other plates is reduced to a total of only thirteen or fourteen. Along each side of the ambulacra was a row of tiny arms (*brachioles*), and perhaps along both arms and ambulacra were tiny tube feet. Typically there was a long, flexible stem of disc-like columnal plates fixed, in some instances, by a root-like base to the sea floor. Food was gathered from (the preferably clear) water around the brachioles and carried to the mouth. The heyday of blastoids was the Carboniferous period after a modest showing lasting from Ordovician time; like so many other benthonic animals, they succumbed during the Permian.

The *crinoids* mark the most successful line of echinoderm achievement among the crinozoa. They have survived to the present day.with over six hundred species. In the accepted manner of their kind, there is a cup-shaped body and a long stem, hence their familiar name 'sea lilies'. The top of the body is plate-covered, has a central mouth and ambulacral grooves which radiate out along the arms. Lining the grooves are cilia which waft food along to the mouth. The anus is between two ambulacra on top of the body.

To capture food more effectively the arms in many species may be branched, perhaps several times, and each branch bears small 'leaves' (*pinnules*), so that it resembles a conifer twig. The stem may have a root region for attachment, but some crinoids have dispensed with the

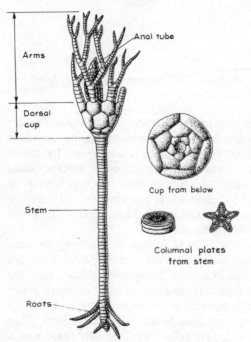

Arms

Anal tube

Dorsal cup

Cup from below

Stem

Columnal plates from stem

Roots

Sea-lilies or crinoids were abundant in Palaeozoic seas: today they are relatively rare. Fragments of the stem abound in some rocks, but the cups are less commonly preserved. Most crinoids were twice the size shown, but some were minute and others gigantic by comparison.

stem and swim by moving their arms or cling to temporary refuge by prehensile 'rootlets'.

Crinoids have an amazing array of shapes and structures in their eventful history. From the early Ordovician onwards they have produced over 750 fossil species. Most of today's species have no stalk but swim in the warmer seas. Stalked types may live 5000 m deep.

The *asterozoa*, the familiar starfishes and brittle stars, are in many ways like stemless crinoids. The mouth and ambulacra are on the under-surface, and the water vascular system opens via a madreporite. In starfish the tube feet are large and powerful and the 'skeleton' of

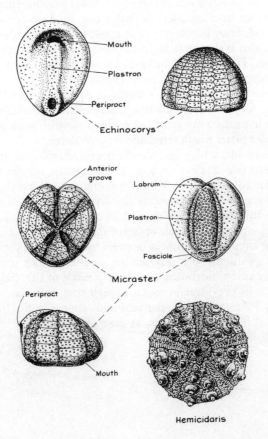

Common fossil echinoids from the Mesozoic rocks of Britain. (About half size).

plates is concealed in a leathery skin so that in modern forms the arrangement of plates is hardly ever seen. Well-preserved fossils are correspondingly rare. Starfishes are active predators among the benthos and are remarkably tough, resilient and vagrant animals with huge appetites.

Holothurians or sea-cucumbers are a much less attractive breed, being cucumber- or gourd-shaped with mouth at one end and anus at the other end of the bilaterally symmetrical body. Some of the tiny podia or tube feet are used for movement, others for respiration. Such 'skeleton' as there is comprises isolated spicules or platelets, and complete fossil holothuroids are very rare. What holothurians have been up to since they first appeared in Ordovician time we can only guess.

The *echinoidea* may be thought of as armless starfishes with flattened or globose rounded bodies, five large ambulacra and immense numbers of little tube feet. The water vascular system is well developed, with a madreporite on the upper surface of the body. The mouth has a novel apparatus of calcareous 'teeth' (the Aristotle's lantern). At the centre of the upper surface is the *periproct*, a constellation of little plates surrounding the anus. Around this in turn are five genital plates each of which has a genital pore, and five ocular plates which terminate the ambulacra.

Fossil echinoids, which include carnivores, herbivores and scavengers, fall into two distinct groups. The Regularia are, as one would expect, strict adherents to a five-fold symmetry. Although they have the underlying five-fold symmetry the Irregularia, on the other hand have, since Jurassic times, developed an apparent bilateral symmetry, becoming elongate, or conical, or heart-shaped or otherwise modified. In some the anus moves towards one end of the body while the mouth changes its position; both stay on the mid-line. Such arrangements undoubtedly suit a burrowing or crawling mode of life. Echinoids are not common in pre-Jurassic rocks, though they may have originated in the early Palaeozoic. Irregular echinoids appear in the Jurassic and are abundant in later formations, as they are today.

CHAPTER 5

FROM WET TO DRY: LIFE ON LAND

LIFE on land and in the air is so universal in the world today that we scarcely give it a thought. Yet clearly life was not always so widespread. Evidence of land animals and flying creatures from the past is not really abundant, despite the great numbers of them that existed through the ages. As we noted in Chapter 1, the chances of preserving as fossils the relics of terrestrial or flying organisms are few indeed. Only when the plants or creatures fall into lakes, rivers or the sea do the conditions arise. Nevertheless, it has been the lot of several phyla of plants and animals to venture into the non-aquatic environments. Plants began the colonization of fresh waters and then the land perhaps even in Precambrian times, as suggested in Chapter 2. By the Silurian period vascular plants had, perhaps, joined the ranks of the terrestrial floras and were changing little by little the character of much of the landscape.

Among the members of the animal kingdom today land-dwellers include protozoa, annelids, molluscs, arthropods and, most conspicuous of all, the vertebrates. Only the insects seem to offer any challenge to the vertebrates as masters of the non-marine environments. Insects are fragile, and only a relatively small number are known as fossils, but they were already around when the first vertebrates crawled out of the water.

All these air-breathing creatures, insect, snail, worm, horse and man, have adaptations for living on land, solutions to the problems of existing without the protection of water. New means of breathing, feeding, moving around and reproducing had to be evolved.

Probably no great changes are required to evolve a terrestrial type of protozoan from an originally marine or freshwater protozoan, but the complex vertebrates underwent a long series of evolutionary changes before they were able to lift their heads on land. Worms burrowing in aquatic mud may have to change but little in the course of evolution to give rise to terrestrial descendants, but with the arthropods rather more is involved. Both the vertebrates and the arthropods have been spectacularly successful in the attempt.

Among the many primitive terrestrial invertebrates one of the most interesting groups is the *onychophores*. They are now found only in the tropics of the southern hemisphere and seem to be 'living fossils', occupying a position halfway between worms and arthropods. As fossils they are very rare, but a few possible specimens have been recovered from a middle Cambrian shale. They all look rather like caterpillars but they differ from true arthropods in having simple undifferentiated segments and simple eyes. Some zoologists regard them as the ancestors of the arthropods and worms. Certainly by Devonian time, or perhaps late Silurian, terrestrial myriapods or centipedes, which are not unlike onychophores, were alive: a few have been preserved as fossils. These little animals had well-developed heads, twelve pairs of legs and several pairs of other appendages like true insects. Perhaps they scuttled around the Devonian vegetation, having emerged from the watery environments at the end of the Silurian period.

The fossil record of the true insects probably begins in the Devonian and is, on the whole, impressive. Insects seem to have achieved their individuality as a group in mid-Palaeozoic time. The earliest lacked wings, but by late Carboniferous time insects were evolved with wings and fewer walking legs. Fossil insects from the Coal Measures show such variety that obviously a great deal of evolution had taken place: insects had diversified into many different kinds, leading different lives. How this all took place is uncertain, but it seems likely that all the winged forms evolved from one basic stock.

An extraordinary feature of insect evolution is their development of a social organization. For example, the bees and the ants have colonies with queens, workers and other ranks. Each has its task and place in the life of the hive or nest. The young are reared in security but most of them grow into workers rather than breeding members of the community. A few Mesozoic and Cainozoic rocks have yielded what seem to be petrified wasp or other insect nests, very similar to the structures insects build today. It would be interesting to know what happened within the walls of those old nests. To account for the way in which this insect organization has come about is one of the most difficult problems in biology.

Of course the insects we have mentioned were not the only ones in the picture. Beetles, butterflies, flies, dragonflies, and many others, are found as fossils. So are spiders, mites, scorpions and other arthropods. Beetle wing cases have been found in some British Mesozoic rocks and beautifully preserved in the peats of the Pleistocene in the English Midlands.

In the *amber* from the Baltic countries there are spectacularly well-preserved insects and other invertebrates. Amber is a golden-coloured transparent substance, prized as an ornament or precious stone, which is in fact fossilized resin from conifers. Insects got stuck in the resin gum on the trees, just as they do today, and now and again amber is found with the bodies of the insects still there.

Slugs and snails, which are locally conspicuous members of the invertebrate land fauna, have a poor geological record. Slugs are gastropods that have given up secreting a shell, but when the familiar coiled house of the snail was discarded by this group is impossible to say. There is reason to think that the first air-breathing gastropods appeared in Coal Measures time, but only in the case of some Cainozoic shells can we be sure they belonged to land snails. There are, however, fresh-water snail shells in abundance in some Mesozoic rocks.

What has just been said is enough to show how uncertain we are of much of the history of the non-marine invertebrates. Yet there are glimpses of them from many geological epochs, and we can be fairly sure that they played a significant part in the background to the evolution of the vertebrates and, perhaps, a part in the evolution of the plants too.

VERTEBRATES

Most successful of all groups of animals in diversifying to colonize an immense number of different habitats, the vertebrates seem to have been evolving at an ever faster rate since they first appeared in early Palaeozoic days. But what are the essential and common characteristics of such a varied group? There are some obvious similarities, and some not so obvious, shared by fish, amphibians, reptiles, birds and mammals. They all have that key structure the vertebral column; this encloses the central line of nervous communication, the spinal cord. The vertebral column is a marvellously engineered structure of blocks of bone and cartilage, or of cartilage alone as in the sharks. It forms around a softer simple rod of tissue called the *notochord*.

At some stage in their life history vertebrates all have gill slits in the body wall near or in the head, and their main sensory organs are gathered at this end of the body, near the mouth. There are other creatures which also have a notochord and gill slits. In the little fish-like creature *Amphioxus,* and in the larvae of sea-squirts, a notochord exists

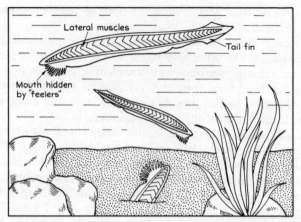

The little lancet-fish *Amphioxus* which often lies half buried in sand is perhaps very like the creatures from which the first vertebrates may have developed. Unfortunately those distant ancestors have left no known record of their existance.

but has been lost in the adult. Acorn-worms, another form of marine life, have gill slits. Although the adult acorn-worm burrows in the mud, the larva is microscopic and swims about by waving tiny whip-like hairs of 'cilia'. It is tempting to suggest that the true vertebrates and these other little animals all had a common ancestor. This ancestor may have had a tiny free-swimming larva with cilia just as the modern echinodermata have. In fact, there is one school of thought that holds the view that these marine creatures – starfish, sea cucumber and sea urchin – may be the particular invertebrate phylum most closely related to vertebrates.

One of the factors that has made the geological record of the vertebrates so full of detail is the possession by these animals of hard fossilizable tissues – bone, teeth, and so on. Bone is produced by impregnation of a soft and microscopic framework of fibres with calcium phosphate. Teeth and other hard parts are also produced by the laying down of calcium phosphate minerals by specially selected cells. In life these hard structures play many parts – as supports, for feeding, attack or defence, etc. After death they may survive long after all the softer tissues have been destroyed. It is a strange fact that teeth which decay so rapidly in our mouths seem to be almost everlasting when buried in the ground.

PLATE 9. Echinodermata are some of the more easily recognised fossils: *above left, Asteropecten* from the Stonesfield Slate, Glos. (× 1) is a fairly obvious starfish; *right*, the 'sea lilies' or crinoids, such as *Onychocrinus* (× 0.8) were very common members of the late Palaeozoic sea floor communities, but are now relatively rare; *below*, the brittlestar, *Ophioderma* (× 1) is from the Lower Jurassic of Dorset and closely resembles modern brittle stars.

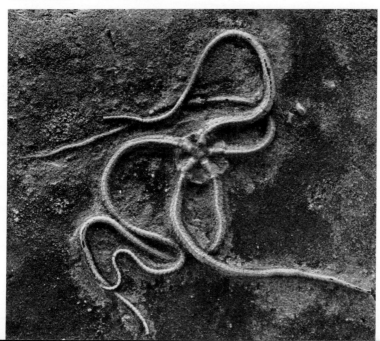

PLATE 10. Sea urchins are common fossils in some Mesozoic and Cainozoic rocks. Here is *above*, the famous *Micraster*, an irregular echinoid from the Chalk (× 1) and *below*, the irregular *Hemicidaris* (× 2) from the Middle Jurassic.

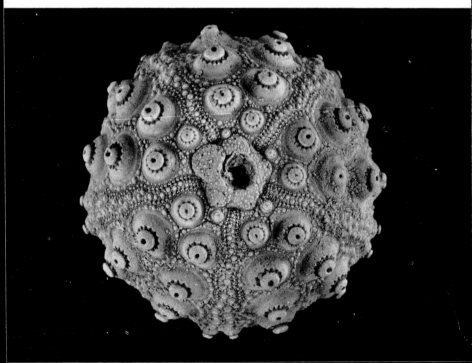

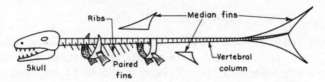

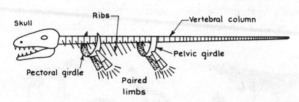

The vertebrates leave behind only their hard internal skeletons (armour in some cases) to be fossilized. Fish (above) and four-legged beasts have relatively complicated skeletons which usually fall apart and scatter after death. (After Colbert).

In most vertebrates the skeleton is a complicated affair of many bones and teeth or a beak, and perhaps a shell or hard bony plates for armour. Fortunately for the biologist, we know enough of the anatomy of modern animals to be able to interpret isolated bones – or even pieces of them – from long-extinct and seemingly peculiar animals. The great Victorian biologist Sir Richard Owen, for example, was once sent a large piece of bone to identify. He was able to say that it was part of the leg bone of a huge bird, standing more than eight feet high, probably wingless and almost certainly flightless, a kind of giant ostrich. No such bird was known, but in due course the complete fossil skeleton of this bird was found. Such Sherlock Holmes-like deductions are not all that rare in vertebrate palaeontology, and one of the fascinations of this science is that new discoveries enable us to conjure up pictures of long-dead animals from comparatively little evidence. It is rather as though, having seen a suit of armour in a museum, we try to reconstruct a picture of the owner of a single helmet or steel gauntlet found on the site of an ancient battlefield.

F.   H

·Pre-Devonian Vertebrates

No one knows for sure how or where vertebrate animals arose nor what their ancestors were. Arthropods, various worm-like creatures and the echinodermata have all been suggested by one zoologist or another as the group from which the vertebrates sprang. Both sea and fresh waters have been thought of as their ancestral home.

Many Devonian fish are found in rocks of a non-marine origin, but pre-Devonian vertebrates have mostly been discovered in marine strata. On balance, it seems likely that early Palaeozoic seas offered

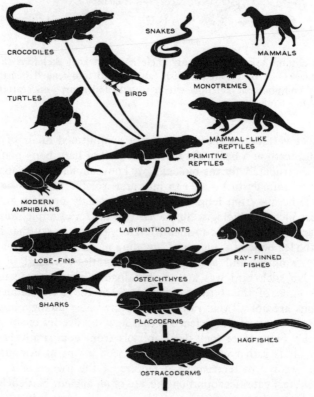

CROCODILES   SNAKES   MAMMALS

TURTLES   BIRDS   MONOTREMES

MAMMAL-LIKE REPTILES

PRIMITIVE REPTILES

MODERN AMPHIBIANS

LABYRINTHODONTS

LOBE-FINS   RAY-FINNED FISHES

OSTEICHTHYES

SHARKS

PLACODERMS

HAGFISHES

OSTRACODERMS

Vertebrates have taken many shapes upon themselves but all are basically fish-like or have evolved from a four-legged ancestor which in turn derived from the fishy stock. The fossil record of vertebrates is tantalizingly incomplete.

the greatest opportunities for the evolution of new kinds of animals. Despite some argument to the contrary, most palaeontologists today think that vertebrates originated from a marine organism of one sort or another.

The first true vertebrates, no doubt, were only a few centimetres long and fish-like in shape. They lacked bones and other hard parts that could be fossilized. The oldest fossils that can safely be called vertebrate remains are from Ordovician rocks. These are rare pieces of bony armour worn by fish-like creatures. It is interesting to see that in these and similar animals in the Silurian and Devonian periods there was more bony material in use as armour for the head and fore-part of the body than as a skeleton within. The calcium carbonate and phosphate salts which were incorporated into tissue to make a hard and rigid structure seem first to have been concentrated more in the outside layers of the animal than within deeper tissues.

In Silurian rocks several kinds of bony plates from these small aquatic animals are known. There are also tiny stud-like fossils, similarly composed of calcium phosphate, which were present in the skin of other small vertebrates. Several modern fish, including some sharks, have such studs, or denticles as they are called, in the skin.

So we picture the earliest vertebrates as small aquatic animals, some of which had a cover of hard parts over at least a portion of the body, others having a more flexible covering of bony denticles set in the skin.

The Age of Fish

The Devonian period was named long ago the 'Age of Fish' because it was during this time that fish became widespread and were the most advanced forms of life on earth. Their fossils have been found on every continent, but are especially well known in Europe and North America. Some of the rocks in which they occur are old lake deposits, as in northern Scotland, or river deposits as in Wales. Nevertheless marine formations have yielded Devonian vertebrates, including sharks and perhaps the largest predatory fish ever known.

Most of these long-extinct animals are known from isolated scales, plates, bones or teeth. Few are found complete, and reconstructing their appearance in life is fraught with difficulties. Only in a few places such as Scotland, Germany, parts of Canada and the U.S.A. and Russia have complete fossil fish been found in large numbers in Devonian rocks. Nevertheless it is clear that in Devonian times the fish evolved into many different groups, some large and some small.

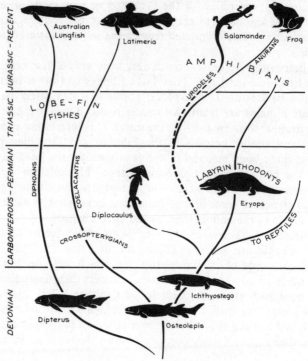

One group of ancient fish gave rise to the amphibia, and so ultimately to the rest of the higher vertebrates.

Their variety was immense, yet by the end of Palaeozoic times virtually all were extinct. The sharks continued to the present day, as did the jawless fishes and the lung fishes and the coelacanths with their limb-like fins. Most of the other existing fish, the teleosts or true bony fishes, first appear in the Mesozoic part of the geological record.

So peculiar are many of the Devonian vertebrates that it is worth noting a few of the kinds that are best known.

The *ostracoderms* were the most primitive. They were small and lacked jaws as we know them in most vertebrates, but had a scoop-like or sucking mouth at or just under the front of the head. They had small eyes but probably used the sense of smell much more, and they were armoured to varying degrees. Most of them may have been scavengers or fed on tiny animals or plants, and many were bottom-dwellers. Few had any paired fins or could have been lively swimmers. Their

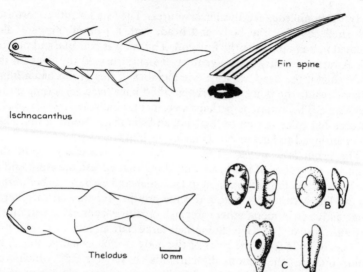

Ischnacanthus

Fin spine

Thelodus   10 mm

A B C

Some of the oldest vertebrate fossils are the fin spines and bony skin denticles of extinct Silurian and Devonian fishes. They are found commonly in several different kinds of rocks but complete fishes are very rare indeed. Here are an acanthodian and a thelodont. The scales, A, B, C, are from different species of thelodont. (About × 8).

armour may have been a defence against predatory creatures such as the larger arthropods or other kinds of vertebrates.

The only descendants of these animals seem to be the modern jawless lampreys and hagfishes which have a parasitic way of life. Lampreys are known from Carboniferous rocks, but the ostracoderms were apparently all extinct by the close of the Devonian period.

The *acanthodians* looked rather like modern fishes in shape and in having several pairs of swimming fins. They seem to have been active swimmers and carnivorous; at least they were equipped with jaws and small sharp teeth. Most of them had large eyes and a useful sense of smell. They had a mosaic of tiny lozenge-shaped bony scales. Acanthodians first appear in Silurian marine rocks, are common in both marine and freshwater formations in the Devonian and Carboniferous, but are not found in rocks younger than Permian.

The *antiarchi* were a very peculiar group of Devonian and perhaps early Carboniferous freshwater creatures. They had a rather tortoise-like shell covering the body and head, with a pair of 'flippers' also encased in bony plates at the fore end. The tail was fish-like and powerful. A rather primitive arrangement of bones formed the jaws on the underside of the head. At least one member of this group had a lung-like sac inside the body and perhaps could have lived for a time out of the water. The antiarchs perhaps were benthonic scavengers who also on occasion came out on to the bank and mudflats. Nothing quite like them survived to later times as far as we know.

The *arthrodires* are so named because of a remarkable joint that connects the plates of the head with those that encase the front end of the body. They too are confined to Devonian and earliest Carboniferous times. The arthrodires were a diverse group, probably all carnivores, some active swimmers, others sluggish creatures content to rest on the bottom most of the time. Some had large flat, almost wing-like projections of bone from the sides of the body as well as paired fins. This group includes the famous dinichthyids or 'terrible fish' which were as much as 10 m (30 ft) long and had enormous jaws. By means of the joint at the 'neck' the whole of the upper part of the head could be raised while the lower jaw was opened. There were no true teeth, but the bones of the jaw had sharp shearing edges to slice through the prey. Arthrodires of this size are only found in late Devonian marine rocks; most were freshwater animals only a few centimetres long.

Sharks and *cartilaginous fishes* are also carnivores that first arrived on the scene in Devonian times. Marine fishes, splendidly streamlined and powerful, they are nevertheless rather primitive as modern fish go. Their skeletons tend to lack the impregnation of calcium salts found in true bones. All that remains of most fossil sharks is their teeth, which are of course very hard, and rare spines that helped support dorsal fins. Some teeth are sharp and fang-like, others are flat or rounded and were used to crush shellfish.

Most of the fish alive today belong to the true *bony fish* group. They are much superior to the ostracoderms and other fishes of the Devonian, but they too first appeared in that period. No other fishes have ever been so successful, so well adapted to their environment. The numbers and kinds of bony fish are legion – they are the most numerous of all the vertebrates.

The first bony fishes were small creatures with rather complex skulls and large toothy jaws, large eyes and a typical 'fishy' shape. They were covered by small, heavy, diamond-shaped scales. In early Mesozoic days they were joined by other similar fishes with heavy rhombic

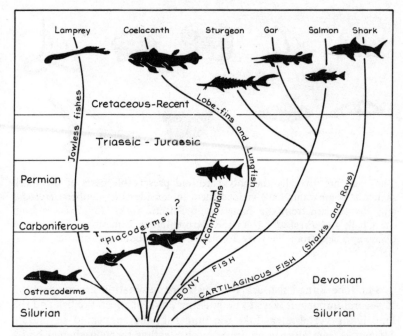

The fishes originated perhaps early in the Ordovician period. Since then their evolution saw remarkable achievements in Devonian time and again since the beginning of the Cretaceous period.

scales, and towards the end of the Mesozoic the essentially modern fish with thin, round scales arrived.

Two kinds of fishes, the *lung fishes* and the *lobe-fins*, remain to be mentioned, and in their ways they are as important as any. The lung fish can breathe air. There are three lung fishes today and most fossil lung fish resemble them rather closely. Two of them can live out of water for months at a time when the rivers in which they normally live dry up. The third, the Australian lung fish, however, can only survive in water though it breathes air when the water is very stagnant. The significance of lung fish is that they show how a group of fish was able in Devonian time to make a 'break-through' – or should we say a 'break-out' – into the terrestrial environment, albeit only for short spells at a time. However, even the earliest lung fish are so specialized that it is unlikely that they are the ultimate ancestors of the air-breathing and four-legged amphibia who indeed made a more effective 'break-out'.

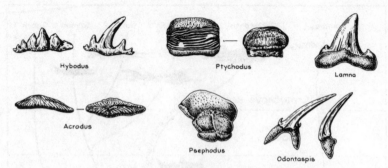

The teeth are virtually the only hard and preservable parts of the shark
skeleton. Some strata have yielded them in considerable numbers. *Hybodus*
and *Acrodus* are from the Jurassic and Rhaetic rocks, *Ptychodus* is from
the Chalk and *Psephodus* from the Carboniferous Limestone: *Lamna* and
Odontaspis are from Tertiary formations. (All about one-quarter natural
size).

The lobe-finned fish are an even more fascinating group, seeming
in several important ways to be 'missing links' between the fish and the
land-living vertebrates. Like the lung fish, they appeared in middle
Devonian time already equipped with a rather torpedo-shaped body,
lobate paired fins and large thick scales. They had bony jaws, plenty
of teeth and a pattern of bones in the skull which set the style for all
the early land-living four-legged creatures to come. The lobes of the
paired fins contained bones which also seem to mark the pattern
which was to be used in the limbs, hands and feet of the earliest
amphibia. For the first time in the record we see a blueprint of a
skeleton which is fashioned much as our own.

Not long ago the lobe-fins were thought to have become extinct
along with the dinosaurs at the end of the Cretaceous period. Then in
1938 a living lobe-fin was dredged up by a trawler off the coast of
South Africa. In the 1950s several others were caught near Madagascar.
The last of the lobe-fins, perhaps, these fish are about 2 m (6 ft) long,
with brilliant blue scales and strong lobed fins. As you may imagine,
there have been few discoveries which have so pleased the zoologists
and palaeontologists. We can investigate in minute detail an animal
thought to have been as dead as a dinosaur.

Out and About: the Amphibia

Out from the weeds at the edge of a Devonian lake or river and on to dry land came the more adventurous of the lobe-finned fish. Though smaller than the first step man made on to the moon, without it there would have been no air-breathing vertebrate to go to the moon – or anywhere else for that matter. Why take such a step? Perhaps drought caused the fish to scramble about in search of more or better water. Perhaps the vegetation and bugs above the water looked more appetizing than those within, or perhaps, though it seems unlikely, there were fierce predators in pursuit.

At all events, the step was successful, and by the end of the Age of Fishes at least one group of fishes had taken it very capably. Fossils from Greenland show us small animals which had four strong amphibian-like limbs, skulls with many amphibian characters and a tail in which the many tiny bones of the fish tail were still present.

So at last a completely new way of life was available to the vertebrates. The plant kingdom had colonized at least the low-lying parts of the land near to the water's edge. The atmosphere had enough oxygen to sustain the rapid chemical activity that the new vertebrates relied upon for energy, and the invertebrate animals had already ventured from water to land. Instead of using lungs only as an emergency measure, the amphibia use them most of the time. Only in their youngest stages did they continue to breathe by means of gills – as we can see in tadpoles today.

No longer immersed all the time in water, the early amphibia had to solve the problem of how not to dry up. A covering of scales may have helped in the earlier amphibians, whereas later kinds had tough skins to keep their body fluids from evaporating too fast. Late in the Palaeozoic era, however, there were amphibia that had become so independent of the water that they only returned there on occasion – perhaps only to lay eggs. Although the amphibia solved many of the problems of how to live out of water they never seem to have devised methods for protecting their eggs on land. They have to return to the water – the old ancestral home – to lay their eggs.

During Carboniferous and Permian times the amphibia evolved into many different shapes and forms, each no doubt representing an animal adapted to life under particular conditions – the coal swamp, the scrubby uplands, the swift-flowing stream, and so on. The environments were many and different and foremost of the inhabitants of each may well have been the amphibia. Some of these beasts became very big and powerful, 2 m long or more. Many died out at the end of the Palaeozoic era: they may have been usurped by more powerful newcomers – the reptiles. Only a few amphibia remain today, specialized hangers-on that have a particular niche no other animal has particularly wanted.

Reptiles Galore

Somewhere in the Carboniferous rocks there may be a remarkable fossil, the first land egg, an egg protected by a hard shell or case. It was an immensely important piece of natural engineering – a sort of space-vehicle or life-support system which enabled the land-living vertebrate to develop directly from embryo to miniature adult without a water-living intermediate stage. In this egg there is food (yolk) and a space for waste products and a porous shell to allow oxygen to pass in and carbon dioxide to escape. With the ability to raise young in this way an animal is free from the need to return to water to reproduce. This was achieved by the first reptile back in the Carboniferous period.

Just how this piece of engineering was first managed we can only guess, but the animals that did it rapidly adapted to their new opportunities in countless ways. Some remained heavy, slow moving; others became light, agile. Some swam, others ran or walked on four legs or two, and some even took to the air. There were smooth ones and horny or scaly ones, reptiles encased in armour or with spikes and prickles. The great days of their existence were the days of the dinosaur, the Mesozoic era.

We cannot give more than a few lines to some of these most fascinating of all fossils, the Mesozoic reptiles. They included many familiar types such as lizards, snakes, turtles and crocodiles and some of them were truly giants, many times the size of their descendants. There was also an abundance of reptiles now totally extinct, the dinosaurs, the marine reptiles such as ichthyosaurs, plesiosaurs and mosasaurs and the flying reptiles pterosaurs. Dinosaurs have always excited the imagination and they were indeed a very successful, varied and long-lived group. They first appeared in the Triassic period and they became extinct at the end of the Cretaceous. Or so most scientists believe, but one of them has been so impressed by the similarities of the skeletons of birds to those of some dinosaurs that he has suggested that in our feathered friends the dinosaurs or their descendants are still with us. Some dinosaurs were as small as pigeons, others were far larger than any other land-dwelling creature has ever been. Some were lightly constructed bipeds, many were heavy and armoured quadrupeds.

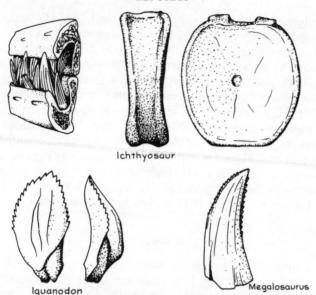

Ichthyosaur

Iguanodon

Megalosaurus

Teeth and bones of ichthyosaurs ('fish-lizards') can be found occasionally in the Lower Jurassic rocks of England. Dinosaur teeth are less common; *Iguanodon* was an early Cretaceous beast while *Megalosaurus* was a fierce Jurassic carnivore. (All about half natural size).

Carnivores and vegetarians can be identified from their fearsome numerous teeth. How did they feed? Were they cold-blooded or, as some authorities now think, warm-blooded? Did they all lay eggs? We have dinosaur eggs and even baby dinosaur fossils hatching from them in Mongolia. And, perhaps most intriguing of all, why did these widespread, large and powerful animals finally become extinct? It may have been for many reasons, changing climate could be one of them.

To match the reptiles on land, large and remarkable reptiles disported themselves in the Mesozoic seas. The ichthyosaurs must have been dolphin-like in appearance, fast swimming fish-eaters who produced their young alive. The plesiosaurs had small heads on serpentine necks and rowed themselves through the water with giant flippers. Other types, again, swam by sinuous movement of their long bodies and possessed jaws of horrendous size filled with dagger-like teeth. With the close of the Mesozoic era they were all extinct.

In the air were the pterosaurs with wings that were of skin stretched from body, arm and enormously elongate single fingers. Some were sparrow size but the largest were bigger than an albatross. All vanished by the close of the Cretaceous period. One group of flying animals, however, prospered. The birds appeared first in the Jurassic period – or at least a 'missing link', half reptile and half bird, is known from skeletons and feathers in rocks of that age. This creature, about the size of a pigeon, has been one of the most discussed and important of all discoveries in the history of the vertebrates. Cretaceous birds were of many different kinds. Many swam, lost their wings but kept their teeth that had been inherited from reptile ancestors. Others lost their wings and teeth and were sea-going, perhaps ocean-going in their way of life. Dinosaurs, flying pterosaurs and sea monsters all became extinct at the end of the Cretaceous period, thereby leaving us a puzzle. In their place came the mammals.

Mammals

Mammals differ from reptiles in many respects, only some of which are seen in their skeletons. (Mammals are warm-blooded, have hair and bring their young alive into the world: none of these attributes can be seen in the fossils.) Many of the characteristics of mammals are found in their limb bones, skulls, teeth and other parts of the skeleton. As surely as reptiles evolved from amphibians, mammals evolved from reptiles. From several places, but especially South Africa, bones and teeth of mammal-like reptile fossils are known, some about the size of a dog. They are mostly creatures which do not seem to have obvious descendants in the next geological era. The reasons for their extinction escape us, but they did perhaps give rise to the first of the true mammals.

The mammals have been the leading group of four-legged animals for the last seventy or so million years. While the dinosaurs were masters of the Mesozoic scene there were heralds of a new order of things scuttling about in the undergrowth. Tiny, but nevertheless genuine, mammals had appeared in the Jurassic period, creatures like the shrew or vole of today. It is not surprising that such small, active creatures have not left behind many fossils, living as they did on land and subject no doubt to all manner of perils. The remains which have survived are rare and therefore precious as relics of the beginnings of the most successful class of animals to inhabit the earth. From several formations in Europe and North America the teeth, jaws and parts of the skulls of four quite different kinds of primitive mammals show that the largest of them was only the size of a cat.

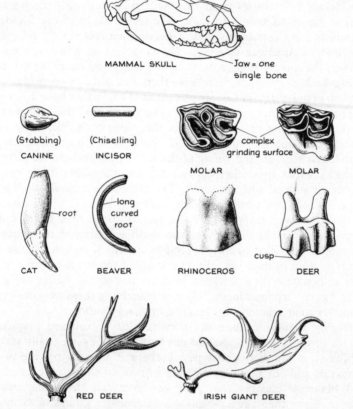

Perhaps the most distinctive remains of fossil mammals are their skulls, horns and teeth. Compared to those of amphibia, reptiles, or birds the skulls have large brain boxes and characteristic teeth. Here are some of the shapes assumed by mammal teeth, and two deer antlers.

But consider what they were able to do. They produced their young alive, suckled them and took care of them to ensure that they survived at least some of the dangers around them. They had efficient teeth and jaws for securing different kinds of food – some may have been insect-eaters, others herbivores and fruit-eaters. We imagine that they were quick-footed, agile, possibly nocturnal. Almost certainly they were furry and had warm blood, and no doubt they produced litters of several young with great regularity.

Cretaceous mammals also are rarely preserved as fossils, and they too include insectivores related to modern shrews and hedgehogs, as well as larger animals with chisel-like teeth. Many of the Mesozoic mammals were marsupials, pouch-bearing animals closely related to the modern American opossum. We cannot be sure that the mono-tremes, the most primitive mammals of today and including the egg-laying duckbill platypus, were alive then, but it seems probable.

Most of today's mammals are placentals. That is, they have developed the placenta – a means of carrying oxygen and food from the mother to the developing embryo. In this way the young (like baby pigs, hamsters or humans) are eventually born as much more developed individuals than are the young of the marsupials such as the platypus or the kangaroo. In another way too they are remarkable, being 'brainy' compared with all other creatures. The placental mammal's skull has a large brain-box in which is a rather efficient brain. For the palaeon-tologist, however, mammals are also remarkable in their teeth, which, after all, survive as the only known fossilized parts of many extinct mammals. And what an array of teeth is known. Mammals have several kinds of teeth in their jaws. From a study of these it is possible to say how and on what the animal fed. In the course of mammalian evolution teeth figure very prominently, and by examining them we can suggest plausibly their relationships and evolutionary history.

During Cainozoic times the mammals have produced a splendid parade of different animals, and this began with a geologically sudden explosion of numbers and types. Perhaps it was the passing of the dinosaurs and other reptiles together with slight climatic, geographical and botanical changes that gave the mammals their long-awaited chance. Since then twenty-eight orders or major groups of mammals have evolved. Sixteen of them exist at the present.

Several of the early Cainozoic groups included very large animals. Some browsed like elephants, others ate grasses, roots or other plants. Early on, too, the mammal carnivores, the cat, dog and other families, made their appearance. Teeth and skulls, limbs and feet, all became modified for various modes of life in different habitats. Eyes, ears, noses, brains, played and play a supreme role in the evolution and success of the different kinds of mammals. Some such as bats now fly, others such as whales, seals and sea-cows have returned to life in water. There are mammals in the deserts, rain forests, plains and pack-ice.

Several great geological events have influenced the development and distribution of the mammals today. The series of great earth movements which has affected the earth's surface since the end of the Mesozoic has isolated areas such as Australia and Antarctica more or less permanently, and other continents were linked by land-bridges from one age to another. Then not very long ago, geologically speaking, came the Pleistocene ice-age with its spread of arctic conditions to many areas that had previously been warm or even tropical. Its effects were great, but some mammals managed not only to survive in the new cold conditions but, like the bear, mammoth and woolly rhinoceros, even to thrive.

Finally, and with a suddenness and effectiveness that cannot have been experienced before in the history of life, has come the impact of man. Himself a mammal, he now exerts an influence on all other forms of life the ultimate result of which is difficult to foresee. The remains of fossil man are among the most rare of all vertebrate fossils, but in Africa and Asia a number of very important bones and teeth belonging to ancient 'ape-men' and primitive men have been found. By geological standards man's history is short and his evolution rapid. He has left a record of his presence not only in buried bones and teeth but also in stone tools and other signs of his activity. The study of these is archaeology, for which we have, unfortunately, no space in this book.

CHAPTER 6

A PATTERN IN SPACE AND TIME

WITH the recognition that fossils are the remains of ancient life, of animals and plants of long ago, came the realization that land and sea are not permanently fixed in their positions but have changed with the years. Fossils give clues as to the conditions under which ancient sediments were formed; and in their evolutionary changes they provide a sort of geological clock, thereby being instructive to the biologist and useful to the geologist. Altogether, fossils have made a distinctive contribution to our study of the evolution of life and the earth itself over the last 600 million years or more. Ever since the early days of geology and palaeontology, however, science has needed to find a means of explaining how rocks, fossils and the modern living world have come to be distributed over the face of the earth in the way they are. Some rather fanciful explanations have been forthcoming, as you may imagine, but the modern concept of how such distributions have come about is perhaps more breath-taking than many scientists of even 50 years ago would have imagined. This chapter will attempt to explain how life in the sea has responded to changes of sea level, the wholesale movement of continents and attendant changes in climate. We shall not forget that on land equally important changes may have taken place as things altered in the marine realm. So we are looking for an explanation of why different kinds of life are where we find them today and in the past, and also an explanation of why some periods in geological time have seen great increases in the numbers of different living things and others have witnessed the reverse, rapid and widespread extinctions.

To explain the distribution of many geological phenomena about the world a theory was put forward in the early years of this century which soon attracted the title of *continental drift*. In essence this hypothesis was that the various continents had in Permo-Carboniferous times all been united and had since then been separating and moving to the places where they now exist. There seemed to be a great deal of evidence to support this idea, but at the same time no one could see how it was that the continents were moved apart. No means of 'drifting' could be found. In the last fifteen years or so all that has been changed and geologists now know that there is indeed a relatively simple but largely hidden means by which the movement is accomplished. The continents seem to be carried about on the

PLATE II. The coiled cephalopod mollusc shells are renowned fossils. In Palaeozoic times they possessed simple suture lines as in *Merocanites* (× 5) *above*, whereas in the Mesozoic era complicated suture lines distinguished the ammonites as in *Harpoceras* (× 1), *below*.

PLATE 12. Fishes in the Devonian period included many primitive armoured forms. The freshwater *Cephalaspis, above* (× 1.2), had a small flat bony head with eyes set near the centre; *Anglaspis, below* (× 3), was smaller but with a distinctive shape and ornament of ridges to its solid bony head covering. Details of the nervous system, gills, eyes etc. can be discovered by study of the impressions on the bone surface.

Geological evidence that the continents have drifted apart since Palaeozoic times is to be found in the matching of the geology on each side of the North Atlantic ocean. In particular, the different geological fold-belts and sediment-filled troughs shown here occur across both areas. We have an early and middle Palaeozoic belt (vertical shading) and a late Palaeozoic belt (criss-cross shading) and four distinct and superimposed phases of geological activity present in both the European and American sides of the ocean. (After Hurley).

surfaces of moving portions of the earth's crust rather like luggage on conveyor belts. The 'belts' are not linnear affairs, but irregular masses, just a few covering the entire surface of the globe. Their movement is powered by terrestrial heat. Occasionally the continents they carry suffer collisions, at other times they are scattered far and wide. All of which has

F.   I great effects upon the evolution of the living things upon and around the continents.

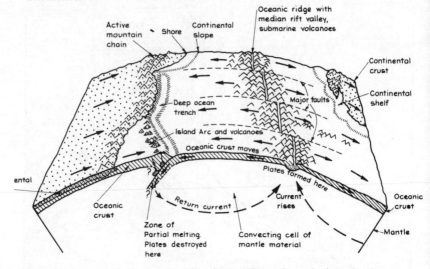

The great geological changes that have taken place during the last 500 million years or so may have been brought about by the wholesale movement of pieces of the Earth's crust. These plates are formed and destroyed as shown above and they carry the continents to and fro on their backs to the advantage or disadvantage of the living world above.

DRIFT AND DIVERSITY

Not long ago two American scientists, J. W. Valentine and E. M. Moores, showed how the diversity of marine life and universal fluctuations in sea level can be related to the way in which the continents have been moved about over the last 600 million years or so. Knowing roughly how the continents have been fragmented, scattered and reassembled over this long period of time, these geologists could explain how so much diversification and occasional extinction came about.

First let us consider what some of the factors are which regulate the diversity or variety of different marine organisms from place to place in the world today. Roughly, there are three such important influences. The first is environmental stability, i.e., the degree to which an environment remains unchanged from year to year or

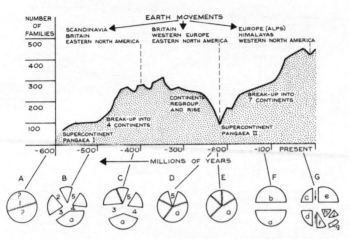

This diagram shows as a graph the levels of diversity of fossils as given by numbers of (Linnéan) families (thick line) and correlates them with the way in which continents have joined together and broken apart.

A, Late Precambrian time, all continents perhaps in one great land mass (1).

B, Cambro-Ordovician time, with breaking apart of "supercontinent" and formation of new seaways (2, 3, 4, 5).

C, Siluro-Devonian time, with N. American and N.W. European continents joined.

D, Late Carboniferous-Permian times bring the continents all together again. The great southern continent, Gondwanaland (a), is joined once more to northern land areas.

E, Permian-Triassic time sees the closure of the last Palaeozoic seaway and the formation of the single great continent, Pangaea, again.

F, Early Mesozoic times see Pagaea split into Gondwanaland (a) and Laurasia (b).

G, Cretaceous-Recent epochs witness the break up of Laurasia into N. America (c) and Eurasia (e); Gondwanaland breaks into S. America (d), Africa (f), Antarctica (g), India (h) and Australia (j).

from age to age so that life can adapt to it. The second is food supply, which needs no explanation, and the third is provinciality, the degree to which a region is in contact with or isolated from other regions.

When all the continents were part of a single 'supercontinent' the marine climate would have had seasonal extremes, because of the excessive heating in summer and cooling in winter of the interior

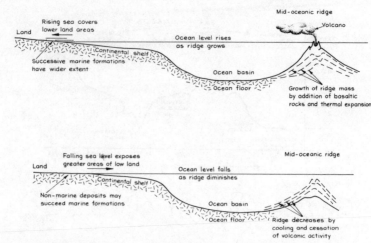

In a geological TRANSGRESSION the seas rise to flood large areas of the continental margins. This is due perhaps to the growth of volcanic ridges in the
ocean floor which displace the water. In a REGRESSION the seas retreat from
the land areas as the volcanic ridges diminish in size. This simple explanation
is only one of several for transgressions and regressions. The actual mech-
anism is probably much more complicated.

lands compared with the surrounding oceans. Offshore winter and
spring winds cause the phenomenon known as oceanic upwelling,
bringing low temperatures and abundant supplies of nutrient salts to
the coastal waters. In summer and autumn the reverse takes place.
Barriers to the longshore migration of plants and animals are few so
that species tend to be rather widespread.

Now if such a supercontinent breaks up, quite different marine
climates develop around the 'daughter' continents. The overall
climate becomes more equable with less difference between summer
and winter and with seasonally more uniform supplies of nutrient
salts in the sea. Under these conditions rather more species tend to
occupy the same areas. As the daughter continents drift apart so their
local species tend to evolve along their own lines and to differ from those
on the other continents. One might say that more continents meant more
different species.

When the several daughter continents subsequently coalesced there
would be something of a return to the original state of climatic affairs.
Once separate groups of organisms would, however, now be brought

into contact and competition. Some would surely become extinct, and extinction would be greatest amongst those groups that were least pre-adapted or least able to withstand the invaders from the other continental margins.

A complicating factor in all this is climatic zonation due to latitude north or south of the equator. The farther a continental coast stretches from north to south, the more its climate will vary and the more its native species will vary in consequence. This seems to be one of the reasons why the world has so very many marine species at present – most of the great coastlines run virtually north-south.

A CHANGING WORLD, EVOLVING LIFE

If we look at the history of the continents and the way they have assembled and dispersed throughout geological time we can be fairly certain of events in the last 200–300 million years but by no means so sure of matters before then. The reasons for this need not detain us here; the figure on p. 131 gives an idea of how this continental quadrille has probably gone on. We begin in Precambrian-Cambrian time with a supercontinent which breaks up only to reassemble in the Permo-Carboniferous. The Permo-Triassic supercontinent did not last long, breaking up into two large 'daughters' which in turn also became fragments. In the course of the last 200 million years or so they have moved into the positions in which we find them today.

During all this time life has been continuously evolving, and, in spite of the extinction of very many kinds of organisms, there has been a persistent gain in the diversity of living things. Nevertheless the rate of evolution has clearly varied from one form of life to another. Extermination and repopulation have been common enough events on the continents and in the seas surrounding them. The cause of mass extinctions have long puzzled biologists and geologists alike. In some instances they can be linked with environmental changes recorded in the rocks but in others we are left wondering. No one today subscribes to the view put forward 150 or so years ago that periodically sudden and violent catastrophes wiped out all life on earth. A succession of creations, each with more complex and diverse floras and faunas and culminating in today's living world, were called for in that theory. Today we concentrate on understanding how life has responded to the local, and the universal, geological changes that have taken place while the continents and oceans have been in motion.

Counting the numbers of different families of invertebrate creatures living on the shallow sea floor and which have left a fossil record in each geological period, we can draw up the graph shown in the figure on p. 131. The rise and fall of the line shows the trends in diversity. It seems to rise with continental dispersal and fall with continental assembly. It appears that the changes in environmental stability do to a large extent regulate the number of species present at any time in the seas close around the continents.

Ocean currents circulating between and around the continents today help to even out the differences of temperatures between the equatorial and the polar regions. This is enormously important in controlling the way in which living things may spread around the earth. The currents, too, carry nutrients from one place to another and help distribute floating organisms. When the positions of the continents change the ocean currents also must be altered and the effects can be drastic. We know that the changes were slow in terms of human experience but on the geological scale they were commonly quite rapid.

From Triassic time onwards the numbers of different kinds of animals preserved as fossils have climbed fairly steadily, with a notable lapse in part of the Cainozoic era when the last ice age was upon us. This is surely a result of the way in which the continents have slowly travelled across the globe to high latitudes both north and south of the equator.

The break-up of a supercontinent into smaller parts occurs when the 'conveyor-belt' system of crustal plates is in action. An essential feature of this system is that the 'belt' is moved away from a line along which new crust is being formed, i.e., where the 'belt' comes up from below. These lines are in fact very largely found in the oceanic ridges which rise like mountain chains beneath the sea. When movement is vigorous the ridges grow in size and when it slows down the ridges diminish – or at least, that is what is thought happens. At the moment the ridges are said to have a volume of roughly $2.5 \times 1000,000,000$ cubic kilometres.

If the ridges were to subside back into the abyssal plains round about them the level of the ocean might be lowered by as much as half a kilometre, i.e., 500 metres, across the entire surface of the earth.

Elsewhere, too, there may be a drastic change in the shape of the ocean floor so that the deep ocean trenches are squeezed out of existence or filled up. This also will affect the capacity of the ocean basins to hold water. When ridges are growing or trenches not very well developed or diminishing the oceans spill over to flood the edges of the continents. New shallow seas are formed over what was land.

When two continents collide further movement of the plates upon which they rest is prevented and the energy within the earth eventually has to find a release by the development of new plate movements elsewhere. There is evidence that once an oceanic ridge ceases to be of use in this way it begins to subside and thus there is more room in the oceans between the continents for more water. The continental seas then slowly retreat to take up the new space back in the oceans.

With these ideas in mind one may imagine that when the continents gather together the seas do tend to drain away from the lands and sea level falls. When the continents split up and move apart they tend to become flooded by the sea. To the delight of geologists and palaeontologists the evidence seems to support this hypothesis. Let us see what the story is that can be read from the geological record and that of fossils.

Life near a Precambrian sea shore is suggested by fossils from South Australia. Sea pens (extreme left), sponges (centre) and algae (right) sprout from the sandy floor while worm-like and jellyfish-like creatures also are present on the bottom or in the water above.

At the end of Precambrian time there was, we believe, an emergent supercontinent. There would have been little life upon its surface but in the shallow seas around it life was undoubtedly quite prolific. In various parts the climate was severe, very cold, with glaciers and continuous frosts. In the seas most of the animal life was of creatures without any hard parts. Few forms would be recognizable to us today but they were worm-like, sponge-like and segmented creatures in plenty, together, no doubt, with many others quite unlike those alive now.

During the next 100 million years or so, the Cambrian period, the great continent split up and the seas encroached upon the land from all sides. In the new shallow marine environments animals began to take on many new shapes and ways of life. Perhaps the most important innovation was the development of skeletons, hard protective parts of various kinds, many

of them made of calcium carbonate. The trilobites swim into pre-eminence
at this time and the various shellfish begin to adopt their first shells. Worm-
like and crustacean animals are also known in plenty. Some of the other
remarkable creatures included the archaeocyathids which set up large
colonies or reefs, together with the calcareous algae on the shallow sea
floors in many regions. These were ideal environments for other creatures
to seek protection or plunder, to feed in or to escape from predators. They
were a far cry from the teeming coral reefs of today, perhaps, but a similar
pattern was established.

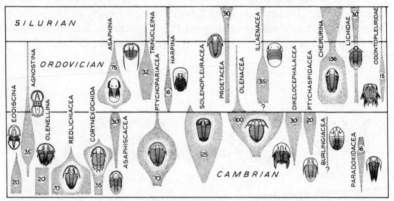

Trilobites were perhaps the most conspicuous animals of the Cambrian
seas but many groups did not survive into Ordovician times. Few groups
survived into later periods, steadily diminishing in variety and numbers,
finally becoming extinct in the Permian period. This diagram names some of
the major trilobite groups, groups which are given different status by
different palaeontologists. The approximate numbers of genera within
groups are given, but there is argument about this just as there is about
almost every aspect of the trilobites. (After Whittington, Harrington and
others).

During the Ordovician and Silurian periods all these marine creatures
flourished, evolved new types and spread into a widening range of habitats.
Some animals no doubt began to explore the lagoons, rivers and lakes apart
from the sea, others perhaps sought security in deeper or colder waters.
The calcareous-shelled animals made great strides, especially the brachiopods and cephalopods. The corals and bryozoa began building reefs on
a wide scale in the open waters of the oceans. No doubt these new structures offered fresh opportunities for other small marine creatures to

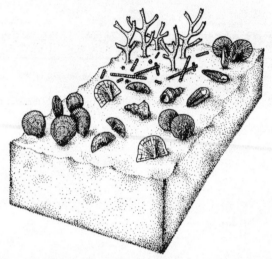

By late Ordovician times there were many different kinds of COMMUNITIES of bottom-dwelling brachiopods and other creatures. Each type of community favoured a special kind of sea floor (sandy, muddy, etc.), temperature, salinity, turbidity and so on. Here is a well-known Ordovician community dominated by *Dalmanella* (D) and *Sowerbyella* (S) but with smaller numbers of *Rafinesquina* (R); trilobites, gastropods, crinoids and bryozoa also present on a sandy floor. (After Bretsky).

develope and evolve. There was a wider diversity of marine life than before. While there were warm regions in which the corals flourished there were also cool areas and parts which at the close of Ordovician time were covered by ice sheets. The growth and decay of glaciers would have influenced sea level and may in part be responsible for extinctions at the end of the Ordovician period.

Plant life began to spread across the land and in the Devonian period vascular plants were probably to be found wherever there was water and some warmth. In Carboniferous times the well-known coal-swamp forests were thriving and complex communities in many areas of the world.

During the middle and later parts of the Palaeozoic era continents began to draw close to one another again and to collide. In doing so they changed the geography of the world in drastic ways. Many of the old shallow seas dried up, being cut off from the ocean, or retreated from the continents leaving behind swampy or arid lands. New mountains arose and parts of

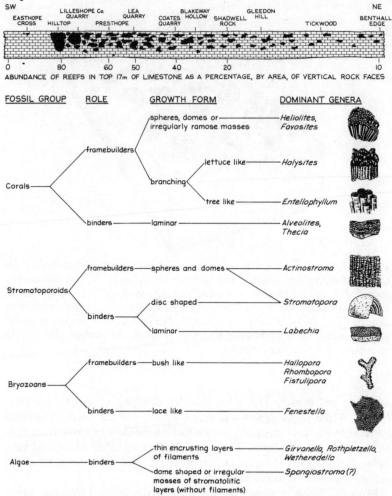

In the Silurian Wenlock Limestone on Wenlock Edge are irregular masses of unbedded limestone (ballstones). They appear to have been formed by the growth of corals, stromatoporoids, algae and other organisms on the floor of a shallow tropical sea. (After Scoffin).

the southern hemisphere grew cold again. These changes were all to offer new environments for the animal and plant kingdoms to colonise and they did so with vigour. During the passage of time competition between

A Silurian *Pentamerus* community
from the Welsh Borderland would
have included abundant specimens of
the brachiopod *Pentamerus oblongus*,
a few less common smaller brachiopod
species, the chain coral *Halysites* and
a bryozoan or two. The sediment
around the animals was largely sand
or silt, giving today fossils in a sandy
or silty matrix. (After Ziegler *et al*).

organisms meant that some groups were more successful than others and
many of those groups that had been secure in Cambrian days were to
become extinct during late Palaeozoic times. The eurypterids, trilobites,
graptolites, some foraminifera and others were amongst those who had

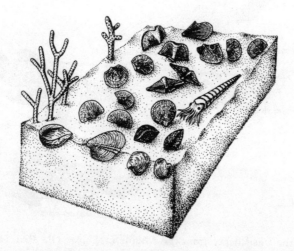

The Devonian period was the great time of the brachiopods and on a sandy
seafloor communities like this may have been very common indeed. The
brachiopods *Atrypa*, "*Spirifer*" and *Schizophoria* are here accompanied
by a few bivalves, two bryozoa and a small nautiloid. (After Thayer).

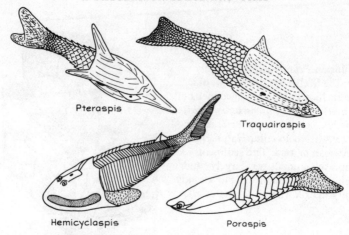

Amongst the strange and primitive fossil "fishes" of the Lower Old Red Sandstone are these bony-plated forms (ostracoderms). For the most part their remains occur as isolated scales and broken plates; complete carapaces are very rare. These animals probably lived on the bottom of local rivers and pools. (About quarter size).

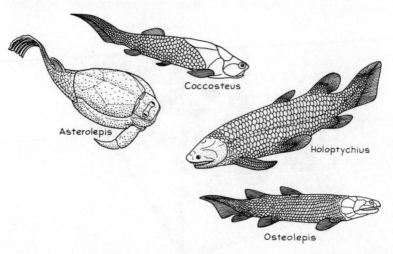

Many of the fossil fishes from the Middle or Upper Old Red Sandstone look not very unlike modern fish. These forms are found in the Old Red Sandstone of Scotland and lived in freshwater lakes and streams. *Asterolepis* and *Holoptychius* could have reached 30 cms or so in length but the other two were only about half that size.

an early heyday and later fell into extinction. To take the trilobites as an example, they provide a good instance of mass extinction at the end of the Cambrian period. Thereafter they continued to diminish in number until the end of the Palaeozoic.

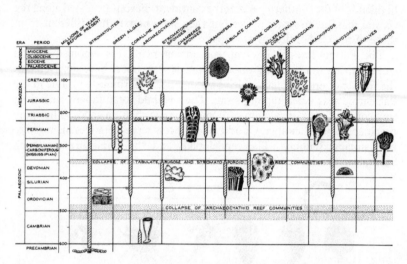

Reef communities take a conspicuous role in the palaeontology of many limestone formations. Since Precambrian days, however, many of the kinds of animals and plants that have dominated in the reef-building process have flourished briefly then declined; others have persisted. In this figure the thin vertical lines show the geological time ranges of the fossils concerned, with the times of reef building shown as thicker columns. The collapse of reef communities seems to have occurred with regressions of the sea (p. 137). A fourth collapse took place at the end of Cretaceous time since when climate has been generally cooler than before. (After Newell).

Amongst the most successful were the early vertebrates. The earth movements of the late Palaeozoic seem to have provided new lands and habitats at a time when the vertebrates were ready to adapt to them with a vigour not seen in any of the lower groups of animals. Escaping, or driven, from the sea, some of them became suited for life in fresh waters and muddy environments, eventually to give rise to the amphibians and subsequently the reptiles and mammals. The world was a busy place in late Palaeozoic days but a sort of nemesis was at hand.

In Permo-Triassic times the continents had swung back together so effectively that a single supercontinent seems to have resulted. A most profound and dramatic change was this, and with it the seas retreated from the continental shelves. The climatic pattern became extreme. Arid deserts were widespread in the equatorial regions while glaciers flowed from the highlands of the southern parts of the continent. Forests persisted along the coastal margins in many places but they were now rather different from those of the Carboniferous swamps.

The Permo-Triassic interval was one of real crisis amongst marine communities. Many large groups of animals seem not to have survived into the Mesozoic era. Animals which had long been enormously prolific in the Palaeozoic seas faded rapidly away. The fusilinid foraminifera with their tiny complex tests of calcium carbonate were such an instance. The spiny brachiopods were another. Of others only a few representatives managed to find suitable habitats. The cephalopods and the corals are two such examples.

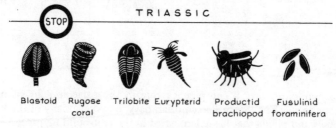

TRIASSIC

Blastoid   Rugose   Trilobite Eurypterid   Productid   Fusulinid
            coral   brachiopod foraminifera

PERMIAN

At the end of the Palaeozoic era very many groups of animals declined and amongst those that became extinct are the forms shown above. Their places in the marine and other webs of life were taken by other animals such as fish, crustaceans, molluscs and hexacorals.

On land, matters were no less serious, for 75 per cent of the amphibian families and more than 80 per cent of the reptilian kinds became extinct by the end of the Permian period. The great Mesozoic reptilian stocks sprang from a few hardy survivors. Things were scarcely better at the close of the Triassic period when the reptile families again underwent decimation. At sea the number of ammonite families suddenly declined from 25 to 1. The single surviving family gave rise to the many of the Jurassic and Cretaceous periods. To find connections between the disappearance of marine forms and terrestrial is not easy, but there may be common factors.

Throughout the mid and late Mesozoic the unhappy state of affairs of the Permo-Triassic seems slowly to have been reversed. The great continent, Pangea, began to break up and to accompany this the seas began to inch their ways back on to the continental shelves more and more. The shallow sea communities re-established themselves once more, but they were now rather different from those of the Palaeozoic. The old shellfish fields were replaced by new ones, brachiopods largely gave way to clams

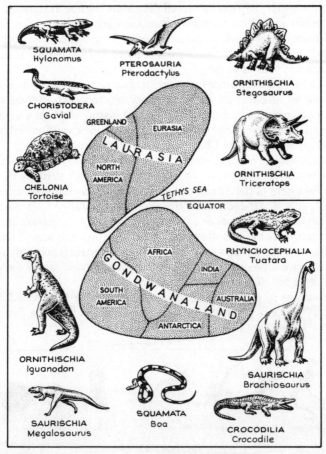

Geological evidence points to two supercontinents existing in the Mesozoic era. Mesozoic fossils from different parts of these continents show that, for example, the reptiles were well spread across each continent. Reptiles seem also to have crossed Tethys from one continent to another via a land bridge or islands at its western end. Here the major groups of reptiles are shown. (After Kurten).

and snails. The corals of the Palaeozoic had gone and more modern forms took over their ecological niches. Palaeozoic plankton was replaced by a probably more prolific Mesozoic assemblage. The vertebrates rose supreme on land and in the waters and in the air. The vegetation had changed but perhaps not too drastically. There is one group of creatures, however, about which we know all too little, yet they must have been very canny, hardy animals to survive apparently so well. These are the insects. Giant dragon-flies, beetles and others are known from the Carboniferous rocks. Smaller but perhaps more varied forms are present in the Mesozoic rocks, but of course insects are rare fossils from rocks of any age despite their great abundance in today's world.

By mid-Cretaceous times major continental break-up was achieved and an enormous spread of sea across the continents followed. In these waters, many of them in the tropics, flourished the marine algae on a seemingly unprecedented scale. Many of them were producers of calcium carbonate – the lime that became the Chalk limestone formations.

Then at the end of the Cretaceous period some of the continental masses began to collide once more. Ocean ridge activity, or perhaps the geo-graphical extent of the ridges, was diminished. There has been something of a withdrawal of the sea, but nothing spectacular, during Cainozoic times until the last million years or so that the influence of the growth and wane of ice sheets over much of the world during this epoch has been to raise and lower sea level by perhaps more than a hundred metres is generally agreed. It would have severely affected the distribution of many organisms, just as would have the climatic changes from warm to cold.

Extinctions in the late Cretaceous period seem to have wiped all but about 25 per cent of the known families of animals from the face of the

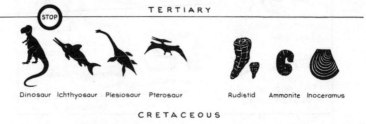

Animals which become extinct at or near the end of the Mesozoic era. Four of the eight orders of reptiles died out and several of the hitherto successful groups of molluscs disappeared. These extinctions were not accompanied by similar changes in the plant kingdom. (After Stokes).

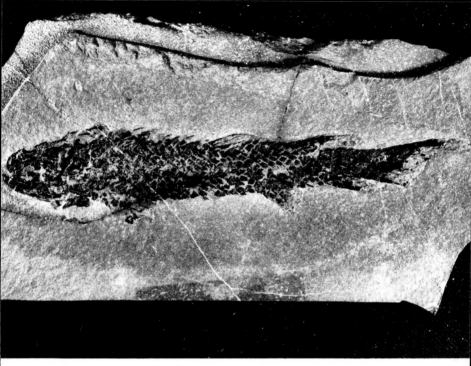

PLATE 13. *Above*, truly fish-like but with thick enamelled scales was *Osteolepis* (× 0.5) from the Middle Devonian of Scotland. *Below*, sharks are commonly represented in the fossil record by their teeth, as they have no true bony skeleton. These are the teeth of *Ptychodus*, a mollusc-eating form from the late Cretaceous (× 0.8).

PLATE 14. *Above*, Mesozoic reptiles include the famous marine 'fish lizard' or ichthyosaurus. This is the head and foreparts with large flipper of a small ichthyosaur ($\times$ 0.25) from the lower Jurassic of Dorset. Also present were the flying reptile pterosaurs, *below*, such as *Pterodactylus* from Germany ($\times$ 0.8).

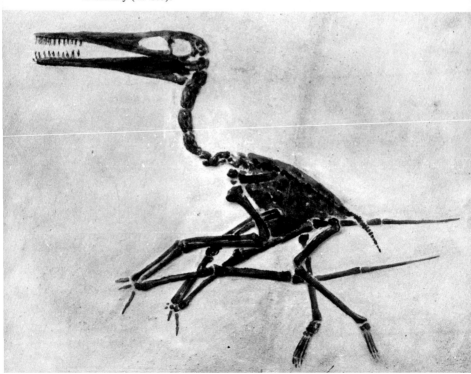

earth. Dinosaurs, flying reptiles, most marine reptiles, the ammonites, many benthonic molluscs and others were eliminated. The plant kingdom seems to have been but little affected at all.

We have tended to concentrate in this chapter so far on examination of the fossil record that is preserved in the marine rocks. But the continents themselves, at least since late Palaeozoic times, have been the scene of biological evolution at its most impressive and spectacular. We look to

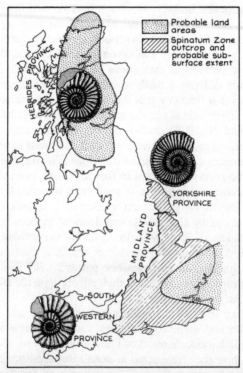

Small but noticeable differences may occur between groups of contemporaneous fossils belonging to the same genus in different places. During part of early Jurassic time there seems to have been three "provinces" for the ammonite *Pleuroceras* in the seas covering Britain. In the South West *Pleuroceras spinatum* was dominant, while in Yorkshire the commonest *Pleuroceras* was *P. apyrenum* and in the Hebridean area *P. transiens* was typical. The reasons for such local distinctions are uncertain but have to be sought for fossils in many parts of the world and of many different ages. (After Howarth).

F.   K continental drift to account for the presence of similar fossil land animals in areas now separated by oceans. Continental separation may effectively isolate whole faunas and floras, as it has done in Australia. Temporary continental connections or 'land bridges' allow groups of animals to migrate from one region to another, subsequently to become separated again. The 'Bering Strait Land Bridge' is an example between Asia and North America. Man himself may have used it.

The last two to three million years of earth history have seen spectacular changes in climate and biology. Mammals have crossed between Asia and North America and its southern neighbour. Extinctions and migrations seem to mark the end of the Pliocene epoch, just as the sharp onset of cold climates in the polar latitudes was becoming felt. Then at the end of the last great glaciation further extinctions of mammals took place. Rather surprisingly they did not actually coincide with the greatest extent of glaciation. From that time onwards there has been a continuous erosion of the numbers of large animals in the world. Many species have gone from Europe, Asia and North America and from Africa south of the Sahara. Climatic changes, principally those from cool and moist to warm and dry, may be the dominant cause of these extinctions. The hand of man himself may not have been very significant in the early days, now, alas, it is.

In all these events the influence of sea level is regarded by many palae-ontologists today as of paramount importance. Coupled with rapid fluctuations induced by the growth and decay of glaciers and ice sheets, world-wide changes of level brought about by the activity of the ocean ridge system were undoubtedly capable of changing the face of the earth and much of its climate and weather patterns. All manner and en-vironmental changes were produced: their effects upon life are recorded by fossils – or by the absence of fossils.

In all the long story of the evolution of the world and its life many factors have operated, some continuously, some from time to time. They are geological, biological, chemical and physical and we are a long way from understanding how they have acted in detail. But these are exciting times for the student of ancient life and the collector of fossils. Old familiar friends, the corals and brachiopods or the fish teeth and scales from local formations, may be seen in a new light. They are part of the evidence of an infinitely complicated and delicately adjusted phenomenon, the passage of life through the geological ages. Without the evidence of fossils the bio-logical sciences would be that much the poorer and we should lack the pleasure of pondering on objects which are commonly as pleasing to the eye as they are stimulating to the mind.

CHAPTER 7

FOSSILS IN BRITAIN

IT has often been said that Britain was the birthplace of modern geology. One of the contributing factors that encouraged this happy event here is the abundance of fossils from virtually every geological period. Certain widespread formations are highly fossiliferous, other quite local beds have become world-famous for their fossils; but of course other sedimentary rocks in Britain are only scant interest to the palaeontologist or are quite barren of fossils. Whether or not a rock formation will yield fossils depends upon the nature of the environment in which the rock material (sediment, volcanic ash or whatever) accumulated and upon the subsequent history of the rock. Metamorphism by heat or pressure are obvious means by which fossils are destroyed, but alteration or recrystallization of the rock by mineral solutions may be equally (or selectively) destructive. Then of course a formation may be deemed unfossiliferous simply because no one has found fossils within it. New methods of examining rocks and their chemistry may reveal hitherto unsuspected organic materials or substances. Keener eyes may find remains where none was previously noticed.

Fossils have been collected from time beyond man's records, perhaps because they caught the eye by their irregular shapes or shelly appearance or because they prompted beliefs in mythical beasts, gods and ghosts. Many of them have been associated with 'good luck' or with the devil, and the folk names given to such fossils are still with us. Naturally enough, it is in those parts where such fossils are – or once were – common that the names seem to have originated. Even as late as the seventeenth century some writers, Dr Robert Plot of Oxford for example, felt that such 'formed stones' had been produced naturally by 'some extraordinary plastic virtue latent in the earth'. Their organic origin was not then recognized.

A few examples of these well-known fossils are given below but there are very many others.

Snakestones	ammonites as in the Jurassic rocks at Whitby, Yorkshire. (p. 75)
Thunderbolts	the heavy pointed internal guards of the belemnite cephalopods, common in the Jurassic and Cretaceous rocks. (p. 76)

Devil's Toenails	the curved fossil oyster *Gryphaea arcuata* abundant in the Lower Liassic (Jurassic) rocks in Britain. (p. 102)
Dudley Locusts	the trilobite *Calymene blumenbachii* found commonly in the Wenlock Limestone quarries at Dudley during the last century. (p. 98)
Delabole Butterflies	the flattened shells of the brachiopod *Cyrtospirifer verneuili* on the shiny surface of the Delabole Slate in Cornwall. (p. 94)
Fairystones	this and other names often applied to fossil echinoids from the chalk or other Mesozoic limestones in Britain. (p. 112)

As we related in Chapter 2, much of the importance of a fossil attaches not only to its form but also to its position in the rock, and its association with other fossils. Thus the collecting of fossils has to be carried out with care in order not to lose such important information. Cliffs, river banks and mountain crags have always been good places for collecting fossils, but quarries, sand pits, road or rail cuttings and other man-made excavations are always worth careful scrunity. Many of the best fossils have come from rocks which were in a partly weathered condition.

A hundred years ago excavations were all dug by manual labour and the workmen were familiar with many kinds of fossils. Since then, although there has been as much if not more excavating going on each year, most of the work has become more and more mechanized and rapid. Under such conditions fossils can no longer be extracted by hand as they once were. Most of them are destroyed in a trice.

The geological map of Britain is a complicated-looking affair, reflecting the complex geological history of these islands. The fossiliferous strata are far from being uniformly distributed but there is, nevertheless, some very real sort of significance in the order in which they occur. This has been determined by the size and shape of the areas in which the original sediments accumulated and the earth-movements and erosion which have since uplifted, deformed and removed them. Beneath all these formations lies a 'basement' of unfossiliferous, metamorphosed, hardened Precambrian rocks: in a few places it now pokes through to the surface or is revealed because of very long-continued erosion. The formations that lie upon this basement fall roughly into two major geographical provinces, separated by a line which runs roughly north-north-east from near Exmouth in Devon to the mouth of the River Tees in County Durham. North and west of this line it is largely Palaeozoic rocks; south and east of it, but with a few errant outcrops on the other side, Mesozoic strata crop out. The Palaeozoic rocks have been affected by a wide variety of upheavals and changes since they were formed. Those of Cambrian, Ordovician and Silurian age were involved in severe compression and changes in what is now Scotland, Lakeland and Wales. Devonian and Carboniferous strata in much of South Wales and south-west England have been similarly changed and folded. Elsewhere they have suffered less but are nevertheless tilted and fractured in various ways.

The Mesozoic and Cainozoic formations have been much less affected, being only moderately or little hardened, compacted and deformed (in mid-Cainozoic times mostly). They occur in a rather regular way in the great scarplands of central southern England and in the vales between them and to the south and east. East Anglia, the Thames Valley and Hampshire appear as areas where the Cainozoic rocks remain in broad downfolds or basins. Quaternary deposits occur as masks of clay, sand and gravel overlying the bedrock formations and can be found in a perplexing array throughout virtually the entire realm in one form or another.

The catalogue of British fossiliferous rocks is a long one, beginning with the Precambrian and continuing to the Recent. In summary we might make a few observations to serve as a general guide to them.

Precambrian formations are often disregarded by most amateur fossil collectors as they have so few obvious fossils. Very rare fossils have been found in Precambrian slaty rocks in Charnwood Forest. Many Precambrian rocks are crystalline, but the sedimentary formations have only rarely yielded genuine (or problematic) fossils which may be of especial interest. For this reason, perhaps, they should be scrutinized even more thoroughly in the hope of new finds. The Precambrian was "The Age of microscopic life" and its fossils are indeed difficult to collect by means available to most of us.

Cambrian rocks occur in North and South Wales, the Welsh Borderland and English Midlands, in Lakeland and north-west Scotland. Many of them, especially the shaly units, have yielded trilobites and other (rare) marine fossils.

Ordovician and *Silurian* rocks are to be found throughout Wales and parts of the Welsh Borderland, Lakeland and the Southern Uplands of Scotland. The Ordovician system includes in addition to a multitude of sandstones, shales and limestones, many volcanic rocks. They originated as ashes and volcanic dusts which locally smothered life on the sea floor. Assemblages of trilobites, brachiopods, molluscs of various kinds, bryozoa, echinodermata and other fossils are common in many such volcanic or sandy beds. In the finer-grained shales graptolites and trilobites may be abundant. There is, however, a snag. Many of these rocks have been distorted by pressure and heat and the fossils they contain are deformed

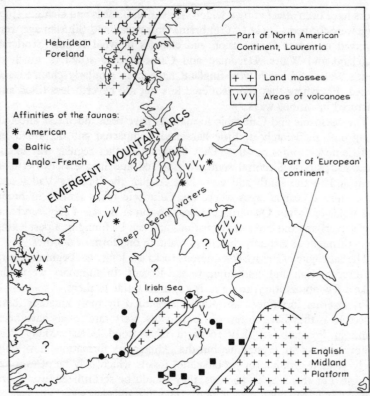

Fossils from certain British Ordovician rocks bear strong affinities to their contemporaries in other parts of the world and may resemble less their contemporaries in different parts of Britain. This seems to be due to the existence of natural barriers to the migration of creatures on the Ordovician sea floor. The slow drawing together of the facing margins of the local Ordovician ocean now brings relatively close together the ancient sea-floor communities that were originally much more distantly separated. (After Williams).

and hard to extract. *Silurian* formations are predominately shaly but thick sandstones and mudstones also occur, and in the Midlands and Welsh Borderlands are found the famous Woolhope, Wenlock and Aymestry limestones. Silurian shales have graptolites and trilobites in plenty while the other beds may be dominated by brachiopods or by coral-stromatoporoid assemblages preserved together with many other kinds of fossils. Silurian rocks in Wales, the Lake District and Scotland have suffered earth-movements and metamorphism to much the same extent as the Ordovician system.

The *Devonian* system in south-west England, too, has been badly affected by metamorphism and disruption but in several areas, especially those where its limestones crop out, it has yielded great numbers of corals, stromatoporoids, brachiopods, trilobites crinoids and molluscs. Elsewhere in Britian, as in South Wales and the Wesh Borderland, the Cheviot Hills and parts of Scotland, the Devonian system is represented by rocks known as the Old Red Sandstone. They are the deposits of rivers and lakes rather than of the sea and the fossils they contain are distinctive primitive fishes and plants.

In the *Carboniferous* system there are basically four great groups of strata. Those in Devon and Cornwall, known as the Culm Measures, are only very sparsely fossiliferous. Elsewhere in England the lower Carboniferous rocks consist of massive grey limestones with, locally, thin shales. Corals, brachiopods, molluscs and crinoidal remains are very common. The overlying strata, the Millstone Grit, are on the whole barren of fossils, but the interbedded black shales may have numerous small cephalopods. In the upper series of the Carboniferous system, the Coal Measures, the commonest fossils are fragments of fern-like leaves and impressions of bark and roots. Rare bands also contain abundant small clams. A few thin bands contain marine fossils.

The *Permian* rocks are generally somewhat unpromising for fossils. Only the Magnesian Limestone on the eastern side of the Pennines has many fossils; they are mostly small molluscs. Some Permian red sandstones have yielded tracks of reptiles while from the Marl Slate of Nottinghamshire many species of fossil fish were once obtained.

The red and green *Triassic* rocks seem to all intents and purposes devoid of fossils. Nevertheless, they have in a few places yielded the brachiopod *Lingula* and a few other invertebrate fossils, some plant remains and rare bones. At the top of the system the thin Rhaetic series contains species of small clams and the worn bones and teeth of fishes and occasional reptiles. The Rhaetic Bone Bed is a widely known instance of a high concentration of vertebrate fragments. Above this comes the *Jurassic* system, one of the most renowned and fossiliferous in the stratigraphic column. Except in parts of Yorkshire and Scotland where the rocks resemble the Coal Measures, its abundant fossils are largely marine. The Dorset-Hampshire coast presents one of the most complete, fossiliferous and interesting sections of the Jurassic and Cretaceous strata. From some quarters of the country, such as Somerset, Dorset and Yorkshire, come many of the famous ichthyosaurs and other marine reptiles.

Cretaceous formations include the sandy Wealden beds of southern England, several other sandstones, clays and limestones and of course Chalk. The Wealden strata locally contain plant remains and were the rocks from which the remains of dinosaurs were first recognized. The Greensand and Gault Clay have long been famous for the beautifully preserved ammonites and other molluscs they yield. Not only famous for its distinctive appearance, but also for the splendid fossils it contains, the Chalk is paradoxically in places a somewhat unfossiliferous rock. Nevertheless, it is composed of ultra-microscopic fossils (see p. 67–68) and various beds within it do yield well-preserved fossils in large numbers. It is locally famous for its sea-urchins, shark's teeth and other remains. The list of the Chalk fauna is a very long one, ranging from protozoa to vertebrates, and indicating a rich array of animals that lived in a shallow tropical sea.

The Tertiary formations of the London-Thames Valley area, Hampshire and the Isle of Wight and parts of East Anglia are also well known for the excellent fossils that have been, and still can be, found there. The London Clay has provided all manner of plants, invertebrates and vertebrates too. Some of the formations in the Isle of Wight also have been very productive. Brick pits, building and road excavations, as well as cliffs and natural exposures, have been of major importance in revealing the treasures of these rocks.

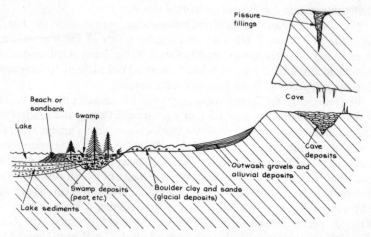

Pleistocene and Recent fossils and subfossils are found generally in the mostly unconsolidated deposits of streams, peat bogs, lakes and glaciers, but they may also occur in caves and even in wind-blown sands. In some parts of the world raised beach deposits may contain vast numbers of bivalves and other shells.

Even the Quaternary deposits, thinly spread though they are, are productive and important to palaeontology. From many parts of the country these sands, gravels and clays have furnished us with evidence of the plants and animals that lived in and around the British landscape over the last two million years or so. This was the era during which ice ages and inter-glacial times alternated and as climate changed so did vegetation and the animals. Glacial deposits have yielded the bones of animals now extinct or removed from Britain – wolf, mammoth, woolly rhinocerus, bear, elk, as well as various arctic-dwelling molluscs and insects. Peat deposits and pollen grains tell us the nature of the flora. Bones and teeth of elephants,

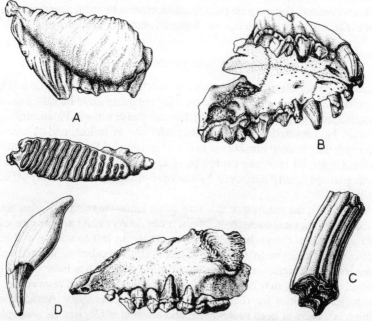

Some of the youngest fossils are found in deposits of Pleistocene or Recent ages which occur in the kinds of environments shown here. The Pleistocene was a time of temporary but widespread glaciations and so glacial age fossils occur close by those in deposits of interglacial or post-glacial ages. Such fossils include bear, horse, mammoth, beetles, plants, snails and occasionally man.

A, Side and top views of the molar tooth of a mammoth, × ·25;
B, Teeth and upper jaw bones of the cave hyena, × ·3;
C, Upper molar tooth of a horse, × ·5;
D, Canine tooth and upper teeth of a cave bear, × ·5;

horses, hyenas and different kinds of deer provide clues as to the inter-glacial phases.

It was during this last geological epoch that many of the cave deposits were formed which have yielded the bones of all manner of familiar animals and of man himself. There is little doubt that many of these remains are of creatures that used the caves as shelter and from time to time dragged in their prey before feeding. On occasion they may have been driven out by cave-dwelling humans.

In all it is a remarkable record of life that is preserved in the many different formations underlying these islands. While new deposits and fossils were in process of formation older fossils were being destroyed by natural erosion. Today a new phenomenon, erosion by student and amateur geologist, not only occurs but has assumed alarming proportions.

A CODE FOR FIELD WORK

Amateur geologists and students now scour the British countryside by the hundreds each year and are responsible for removing quite literally tons of material from the field to their homes, laboratories or schools. Palaeontology, it must be admitted, appeals to those who like to collect, and of course there are only limited numbers of fossils to go round. Many localities which yielded splendid specimens some years ago are now barren, worked out, even perhaps totally destroyed by the over-enthusiastic or simply selfish collectors.

Apart from the annoyance this may cause landowners, quarrymen and subsequent visitors in search of fossils, it can do very real harm as rare and beautiful material may be destroyed or otherwise lost to science and the provision of enjoyment to many. Thus a large number of learned and conservation societies, clubs, museums and other bodies have begun to consider how they may help to conserve our palaeontological resources and geological localities for the benefit of all. The Geologists' Association, which is a body of both professional and amateur geologists, for example, has set out a code for geological field work.

Many of the points in this code are those which anyone familiar with the Country Code would naturally observe. Where collecting specimens is concerned the Association is anxious that students should be encouraged to observe but not to use their geological hammers indiscriminately and it adds 'KEEP COLLECTING TO A MINIMUM. Avoid removing *in situ* fossils, rocks or minerals (this is, those still in the solid rock) unless they are genuinely needed for serious study . . . The collecting of actual specimens should be restricted to those localities where there is a plentiful supply, or to a scree, fallen blocks and waste tips . . . Never collect from walls or buildings. Take care not to undermine fences, walls, bridges or other structures'. To which might be added 'remember the next person and do not be greedy'.

It is suggested that everyone can help by fostering an interest in geological sites and their wise conservation. Schools and other bodies are urged to remember that much may be done by collective effort to help clean up over-grown sites (with permission of the owner and in consultation with the Nature Conservancy Council). Contact with the local County Naturalists' Trust, Field Study Centres, Natural History Societies or Museums will help to ensure that there is co-ordination in attempts to conserve geological sites and to retain access to them. All the organizations mentioned seek to help everyone enjoy geology, to learn from it and to ensure that future generations will be able to do so too. Each individua l has his responsibilities in the field.

BRASS TACKS

Bearing all this in mind, there is no reason why one should not collect fossils out of genuine interest, and in the hope that something new may be added to science. Fossils put away and seen only occasionally by one pair of eyes are probably fossils lost to science. Here are some tips about the business of actually collecting fossils in the field and building a collection.

Useful equipment includes a hammer, a chisel or two, maybe a small brush tó clear away chippings, a hand lens and various materials for packing and carrying specimens: some glue, cotton wool, a box or two of phials for small objects and paper for wrapping larger items are also necessary. Paper or cloth bags to hold specimens are very useful.

No one should collect specimens without making a note of *exactly* where the fossil occurred, and no fossil should be taken without being labelled so that it can always be related to its point of origin. Thus a felt tip pen for marking specimen or package and a field note book for recording occurrences are very important.

Many a good fossil is spoilt by the finder's attempts to remove it from the rock. If it is small enough to be broken off together with some of the enclosing matrix well and good, but the careful use of hammer and chisel may be necessary. Use the natural 'grain' of the rock if possible and make sure that a good margin is preserved between chisel and fossil. It may be necessary to protect the fossil by wet paper, mud or plaster while you attack the rock. Collected specimens must be carefully wrapped and carried home. They can suffer damage by bumping together in a rucksack.

In many instances fossils can be retrieved from muds or sands by simple sieving or panning to wash away the mud or mineral grains.

Once home, the collected specimens may be washed or scrubbed with a

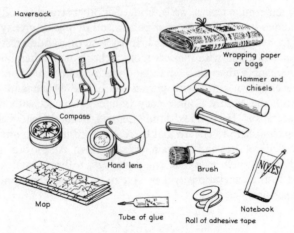

The simplest and cheapest equipment for collecting fossils is often the most useful. Many good specimens have been ruined after they have been found by careless removal from the rock and by rough treatment between field and specimen drawer. Equally important for all fossil collecting forays is the permission of the landowner on whose property the fossils may occur, and an exact record of where the fossils are found.

soft brush, matrix may be delicately removed by using small chisels or a pin vice to hold a steel needle or pick. To preserve fragmenting material glue or varnish can be applied and in some instances acid can be used to remove a limestone matrix. Acid is nasty stuff to handle, and should only be used in very diluted form; acetic or hydrochloric acids are most commonly used. Weak acetic acid can be used for extracting bones, teeth and other phosphatic fossils from limestones, but hydrochloric acid attacks even these hard materials. Seek further advice if possible before attempting to use acid as an aid in cleaning specimens or dissolving rock.

Finally the palaeontologist needs to house his specimens in small boxes or cardboard trays, or in phials to protect them. Specimen and label should have a common reference number and the rock formation and locality must be recorded. A fossil may lack a name but it should never lack an address: very many fossils have lost much of their value because the details of where they were found have been mislaid. Putting a name to the species collected is not easy in most cases. Books, museums and helpful friends or specialists should be consulted wherever possible. A good collection can give hours of pleasure as well as something of value to science but it requires for its making, patience and care, knowledge and not a little sheer luck.

FOSSILIFEROUS BRITAIN

Fossiliferous formations are widespread throughout the British Isles, except in the highlands of Scotland and parts of Ireland. Descriptions of the rocks and their fossils are to be found in very many journals and periodicals as well as in numerous books. The *Memoirs* and the *British Regional Geology* handbooks of the Institute of Geological Sciences give local details and broad outlines respectively. *Stanford's Geological Atlas of Great Britain* (2nd edition 1964) is another source of information; but perhaps the best geological guides to many parts of the country have been provided by the Geologists' Association in its *Proceedings* and its Guides to the Geology of Classical Areas and around University towns since 1954 (obtainable from Benham & Co., Ltd., Sheepen Road, Colchester, at modest prices).

On our simplified geological maps of the British Isles the geological regions and a few of the salient formations are outlined and some notes about these are given below.

KEY TO MAPS ON PAGES 158-165

Tertiary formations

The Chalk and Upper Greensand

Jurassic and Lower Cretaceous

New Red Sandstone

Carboniferous

Lower Palaeozoic and Devonian

Precambrian and all igneous rocks

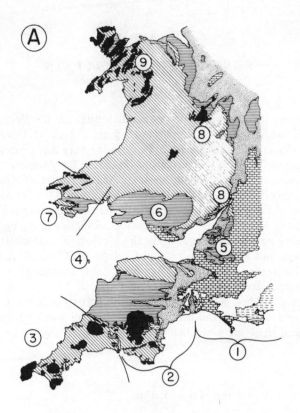

(A)

1. The Dorset coast. Famous and highly fossiliferous cliffs along this coastline are described in *British Regional Geology: The Hampshire Basin and Adjoining Areas*. H.M.S.O. 3rd Edition, 1960.
The Dorset Coast. G. M. Davies, A. & C. Black, London, 2nd Edition 1956.
Geological Highlights of the West Country. W. A. Macfadyen. Butterworth, London, 1969.

2. South Devon has many fossiliferous localities as described in *British Regional Geology: Southwest England*. H.M.S.O. 4th edition, 1975.
Geology Explained in South and East Devon. J. W. Perkins. David and Charles, Newton Abbot, 1971.

3. The Devonian rocks of Cornwall are only locally and somewhat sparsely fossiliferous. Apart from the sea cliffs, exposures of fossil-bearing rocks are not common.

4. The Culm Measures (Carboniferous) and Devonian rocks of N. Cornwall and N. Devon locally contain fossils but these are difficult to extract and many have been deformed by pressure.

5. The Mendip area yields both Carboniferous and Jurassic fossils in abundance and there are many quarries in the Cotswolds which reveal fossiliferous rocks. See
British Regional Geology: The Bristol and Gloucester District. H.M.S.O. 2nd edition, 1948.
Geology Explained in the Severn Vale and Cotswolds. W. Dreghorn. Davis and Charles, Newton Abbot, 1967.
Geological Highlights of the West Country. W. A. Macfadyen. Butterworth, London, 1969.
The Geology of Wiltshire. R. S. Barron, Moonraker Press, Bradford on Avon, 1976.
Geological Excursions in the Bristol District. Edit. R. J. G. Savage, University of Bristol, 1977.

6. The Forest of Dean Coalfield and the South Wales Coalfields have long been known for the plant remains from their Coal Measures and for the brachiopods, corals and other marine fossils from the Carboniferous Limestone that rims these coalfields
British Regional Geology: South Wales. H.M.S.O. 3rd edition, 1970.
Geology Explained in the Forest of Dean and the Wye Valley. W. Dreghorn. David and Charles, Newton Abbot, 1968.

7. Dyfed's (Pembrokeshire) cliffs and beaches expose fossiliferous formations of many ages from Cambrian to Carboniferous.
Geological Excursions in S. Wales and the Forest of Dean. Geologists' Assoc., S. Wales Group, Cardiff, 1971.

8. The Welsh Borderland, principally southern Shropshire and Worcester and Herefordshire, includes the classical fossiliferous localities of the Silurian system and other Palaeozoic formations. *British Regional Geology: The Welsh Borderland.* H.M.S.O. 3rd edition, 1971.

9. North Wales presents a wide array of sedimentary and igneous rocks of Palaeozoic age but fossils are not everywhere easy to find, despite the splendid exposures on coasts and mountains.
British Regional Geology: North Wales. H.M.S.O. 3rd edition, 1971.

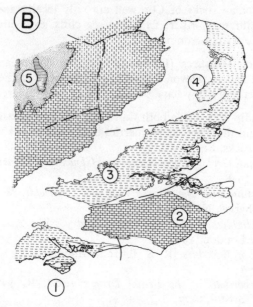

(B)

1. The Hampshire Basin is that region lying south of the Chalk downlands of Hampshire and this area together with the Isle of Wight offers many opportunities to collect from the Cretaceous and Tertiary rocks.
British Regional Geology: the Hampshire Basin and Adjoining areas. H.M.S.O. 3rd edition, 1960.

2. The Weald and adjacent areas, the North and South Downs, are almost exclusively formed of Cretaceous rocks. Some of the Wealden sandstones and clays are fossiliferous while the Gault, Greensands and Chalk exposed on the coastline are renowned for their fossils.
British Regional Geology: The Wealden District. H.M.S.O. 4th edition, 1965.

3. Fossiliferous exposures of Jurassic, Cretaceous and Tertiary formations in the Thames valley area are numerous but scattered and many are only of a temporary nature. Large chalk quarries and pits in the London Clay are exceptions. A good overall account is given in *British Regional Geology: London & Thames Valley.* H.M.S.O., 3rd edition, 1960, and in *Geology of London and South East England* by G. M. Davies, Murby & Co., London 1939.

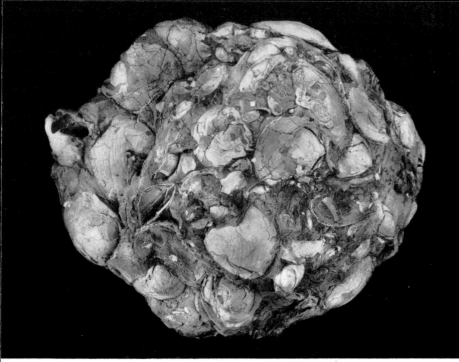

PLATE 15. *Above*, fossils may locally occur in clusters cemented tgether by mineral matter much harder than the local rock. Such a concretion is this one containing the clam *Glycimeris* (× 0.3) from the London Clay of Sussex. *Below*, a Lower Jurassic 'shell bed' with the large heavy shells of *Gryphaea* and many other smaller kinds (× 0.5) from Dorset.

PLATE 16. *Above*, seemingly unfossiliferous Old Red Sandstone beds at Portishead, Avon, which have nevertheless yielded several different kinds of fossil fishes from the fine red layers between the more massive beds. *Below*, large old quarry workings at Chipping Sodbury, Avon, where the fossiliferous steeply dipping Carboniferous Limestone are overlain by horizontal fossiliferous beds of shale and limestone of Triassic age. Old quarries are commonly good localities for fossils but they may be private property and they may be in a dangerous condition.

4. East Anglia and the county south of The Wash is rather flat and, except in a few large quarries and on the coast, little of the geology is exposed. It is however the one area famous for the Pliocene "Crag" deposits which include many species of (well preserved) molluscs. *British Regional Geology: East Anglia and Adjoining Areas* H.M.S.O., 4th edition, 1961.

5. The English Midlands is rich in fossiliferous rocks of almost all ages from Cambrian to late Jurassic. Many of these formations occur in quarries and pits for economic rock materials. *British Regional Geology: Central England* H.M.S.O., 3rd edition, 1969.

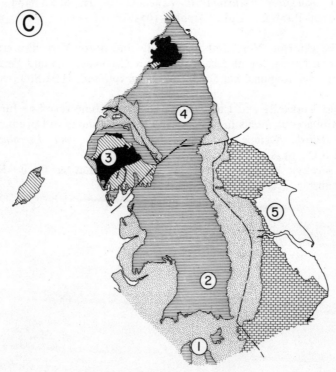

(C)

1. The northern part of the English Midlands extends into this map area.

2. The Pennines range is famous for its Carboniferous Limestone

F.   L

fossils and of course there are others locally common in the shales of the Millstone Grit and the Coal Measures (especially plants).
British Regional Geology: the Pennines and Adjacent Areas, H.M.S.O., 3rd edition, 1954.
Geology explained in the Peak District. F. Wolverson Cope,' David & Charles, Newton Abbot, 1976.

3. Lakeland has many fossiliferous strata within its crags and scarps. Lower Palaeozoic formations are locally very fossiliferous, as is the Carboniferous Limestone, the local Coal Measures and some of the Permian rocks.
British Regional Geology: Northern England, H.M.S.O., 4th edition, 1971; *Geological Excursions in Lakeland*, E. H. Shackleton, The Dalesman Publ. Co. Ltd., Clapham 1975.

4. The Cheviot, Northumberland Fells and north Yorkshire area is also well-known for its locally abundant Carboniferous and Permian fossils. (See Regional handbook: *Northern England*, H.M.S.O., 1971).

5. East Yorkshire and Lincolnshire has given some very fine Jurassic and Cretaceous fossils in the past and the coastline is still productive. See *British Regional Geology: East Yorkshire and Lincolnshire*, H M S O , 1948.
The Geology of Lincolnshire, H. H. Swinnerton & P. E. Kent, Lincolnshire Nationalists' Union, 1976.

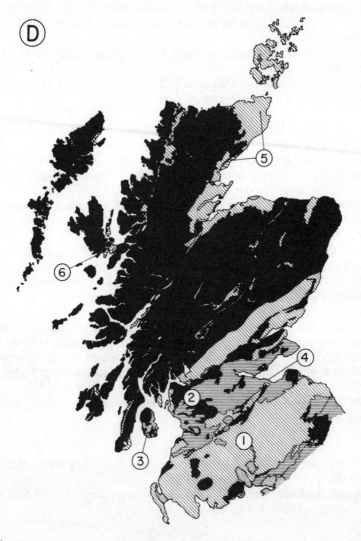

(D)

1. The southern uplands of Scotland are primarily given over to Ordovician and Silurian rocks, locally very fossiliferous, but on northern and southern flanks Carboniferous beds are also present. *British Regional Geology: South of Scotland*, H.M.S.O., 2nd edition, 1948.

2. Clydeside and the Glasgow area lie within the great Midland Valley of Scotland with its many fossiliferous formations, notably of Carboniferous age.
British Regional Geology: Midland Valley of Scotland, H.M.S.O., 2nd edition, 1948.
Geology explained around Glasgow and Southeast Scotland, J. D. Lawson; David & Charles, Newton Abbot, 1976.

3. The Isle of Arran is a remarkable storehouse of geological formations, with fossils to be found principally in the Carboniferous rocks.
Excursion Guide to the Geology of Arran. Murray MacGregor with contrib. by A. Herriot and B. C. King. Geol. Soc. of Glasgow, 1955.

4. The Edinburgh region also lies within the geological province of the Midland Valley of Scotland.
The Geology of the Lothians and S. E. Scotland.
G. Y. Craig & P. McL. D. Duff (Eds.) Edinbugh Geological Society: Scottish Academic Press, Edinburgh, 1975.
Fife & Angus Geology: An Excursion Guide, A. R. McGregor, Scottish Academic Press, 1968.

5. Along the north-eastern coastline of Scotland and in the Orkney and Shetland Islands Devonian rocks have long been famous for their fossil fish. Jurassic coals also occur at Brora on this coastline.
British Regional Geology: Northern Highlands, H.M.S.O., 3rd edition, 1960.
The Caithness Book. D. Omand (edit.) Highland Printers Ltd., Inverness, 1972.

6. Small areas of Jurassic rocks containing fossils are found in Skye and elsewhere in the Inner Hebrides.
British Regional Geology: Tertiary Volcanic Districts, H.M.S.O., 3rd edition, 1961.

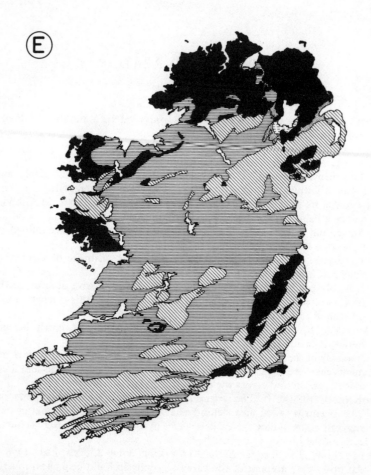

(E)

(E)
The Irish geological map is dominated by the Lower Carboniferous
and the Carboniferous Limestone and associated Millstone Grit beds
have yielded many beautiful fossils. The coastline offers especially
good opportunities for collecting.

British Regional Geology: Northern Ireland, H.M.S.O. 1972.
Geology and Ireland by W. E. Nevill, Allen Figgis & Co., Dublin, 1963.
Historical Geology of Ireland by J. K. Charlesworth, Oliver & Boyd,
Edinburgh, 1963.
Geology and Scenery in Ireland by J. B. Whittow, Penguin Books, 1974.

BOOKS TO READ

SOME GEOLOGICAL BACKGROUND is provided in a number of books which are not too technical or expensive.

CALDER, N. *Restless Earth* B.B.C. Publications, 1972.
The printed version of a spectacular TV programme. Readable and splendidly illustrated, mostly concerned with continental drift.

DINELEY, D. L. *Earth's Voyage Through Time*. Hart Davis McGibbon, and as a Paladin Paperback, Granada Publ. Ltd., 1975.
An account of the earth's history and the processes which have influenced it, written for the layman.

GEOLOGICAL MUSEUM. *The Story of the Earth*. Institute of Geological Sciences, London 1972.
A highly condensed but extremely useful and impressive account of the processes that have influenced the evolution of this planet. Fully illustrated.

LAPORTE, L. A. *Ancient Environments*. Foundations of Earth Science Series, Prentice-Hall Inc., 1968, 2nd ed., 1977.
A survey of the means by which we are able to distinguish what environments gave rise to the many different kinds of sedimentary rocks and fossil assemblages found across the continents today.

PONNAMPERUMA, C. *The Origins of Life*. Thames & Hudson, 1972.
The chemistry that lies behind the formation of living matter and suggestions as to how the various stages in the origin of life were achieved early in the history of the earth.

WYLLIE, P. *The Way the Earth Works*. John Wiley & Sons, Ltd., 1976.
An up-to-date account of the various geophysical and geological investigations that have led to the model of the earth's behaviour that many geologists hold today.

GENERAL ASPECTS OF PALAEONTOLOGY are dealt with in several excellent textbooks: there are also numerous popular books of which the following few are worthy of note:-

BEERBOWER, J. R. *Search for the Past: An Introduction to Palaeontology*. Prentice-Hall (2nd ed.) 1968.
Essentially a textbook for American students, written in a rather racy fashion but well worth browsing through.

BLACK, R. M. *The Elements of Palaeontology.* Cambridge University Press, 1970.
A general text for students, perhaps the best such British book on the market.

BROUWER, A. *General Palaeontology.* Oliver & Boyd, 1967.
A discussion of the many different problems and aspects that palaeontology presents to scientists at large.

CHARIG, A. & HORSEFIELD, B. *Before the Ark.* B.B.C. Publications, 1975.
A fascinating account of palaeontology as given in a popular television series.

CLARK, D. L. *Fossils, Palaeontology and Evolution.* W. G. Brown Co., 1968.
A short text relating these items to one another and discussing the contribution that palaeontology has made to our modern view of evolution.

COWEN, R. *The History of Life.* McGraw-Hill, Ltd., 1976.
A somewhat cursory account of this topic.

FENTON, C. L. & FENTON, M. A. *The Fossil Book.* Doubleday and Co. Inc., 1958.
A large and lavishly illustrated book which every amateur palaeontologist should try to see.

HAMILTON, R. *Fossils and Fossil Collecting.* Hamlyn all-colour paperbacks, 1975.
An ideal book for the amateur palaeontologist; pocket-sized, and useful to have with one in the field.

HAMILTON, R., WOOLEY, A. R., & BISHOP, A. C. *The Hamlyn Guide to Minerals, Rocks and Fossils.* Hamlyn, 1974.
A rather fuller and splendidly illustrated guide which is perhaps the best on the market at the moment. In all respects excellent.

KIRKALDY, J. F. *The Study of Fossils.* Hutchinson, 1963.
A brief introduction to palaeontology, somewhat dated in its approach.

KIRKALDY, J. F. *Fossils in Colour.* Hamlyn.
A very useful pocket guide to fossils, especially those in Britain.

MCALESTER, A. L. *The History of Life.* Foundation of Earth Science Series. Prentice-Hall, 1968.
Another well-illustrated and excellently written volume in the Foundations of Earth Science Series. Heartily recommended.

MIDDLEMISS, F. A. *A Guide to Invertebrate Fossils.* Hutchinsons Educational Series, 1968.

OAKLEY, K. P. & MUIR-WOOD, H. M. *The Succession of Life through Geological Time.* British Museum (N.H.), 1964.
A somewhat straight-laced account, but good, of fossils and the history of life they reveal.

PINNA, G. *The World of Fossils.* Orbis Publ. Ltd., 1975.
Recommended for its beautiful photographs of fossils, but not so impressive in its text. A book for collectors of fossils – and books.

RHODES, F. H. T., ZIM, H. S., SHAFFER, P. S. *Fossils: A Guide to Prehistoric Life.* Hamlyn paperbacks, 1965.
Many excellent coloured illustrations in a little book principally intended for the American amateur fossil collector.
SCOTT, J. *Palaeontology: An Introduction.* Khan and Averill, 1973.
A text which covers much the same broad ground as the books by Brouwer and Black, well written, but poorly illustrated.
SWINNERTON, H. H. *Fossils.* Collins New Naturalist Series, 1960.
A general account and something of a classic, but also rather dated.

MORE SPECIALIZED, though not necessarily more technically written books on palaeontology include the following:-

COLBERT, E. H. *The Age of Reptiles.* Wiedenfield & Nicholson, 1965.
COLBERT, E. H. *Men and Dinosaurs.* Penguin Books, 1968
COX, C. B. *Prehisoric Animals.* Hamlyn all-colour paperbacks, 1969.
DAY, M. H. *Fossil Man.* Ibid., 1975.
ROMER, A. S. *The Procession of Life.* Wiedenfield & Nicholson, 1968.
SWINTON, W. E. *Dinosaurs.* British Museum (N.H.), 1964.
SWINTON, W. E. *Fossil Amphibia and Reptiles.* Ibid., 1965.
SWINTON, W. E. *Fossil Birds.* Ibid., 1958.

The BRITISH MUSEUM (NATURAL HISTORY) has issued three books illustrating common British Fossils. They are very useful for students and for anyone interested in collecting fossils from some of the classical areas in Britain. Now in their fifth editions, they are:-

> *Palaeozoic Fossils,* (1964)
> *Mesozoic Fossils,* (1962)
> *Cainozoic Fossils,* (1959)

TEXTBOOKS of the more advanced and technical kind have been published more frequently in Europe or North America than in Britain. Hence the majority of those listed below are from the United States. Naturally, they refer mostly to North American species and they may not be easy to find in the U.K.
AGER, D. V. *Principles of Palaeoecology.* McGraw-Hill Book Co. Inc., 1963.
A useful introduction to the subject but perhaps not for the beginner.
MOORE, R. C. (Editor). *Treatise on Invertebrate Palaeoentology.* Geological Society of America and Kansas University Press, 1953.
A reference work in many volumes dealing with all the phyla of fossil invertebrates. Almost every known genus is mentioned or described.
MOORE, R. C., LALICKER, C. G. & FISCHER, A. G. *Invertebrate Fossils.* McGraw-Hill Book Co. Inc., 1952.
Another large and well-illustrated text for university students.

RIXON, A. E. *Fossil Animal Remains: Their Preparation and Conservation.* Athlone Press, 1976.
A useful book for the professional or most ardent enthusiast who has some vertebrate material in his collections.

STANLEY, S. M. & RAUP, D. M. *Principles of Palaeontology.* W. H. Freeman & Co., 1971.
A very well produced book, primarily intended for university students.

SHROCK, R. R. & TWENHOFEL, W. H. *Principles of Invertebrate Palaeontology.* McGraw-Hill Book Co. Inc., 2nd edition, 1953.
For many years this was the standard palaeontology book for university students.

TASCH, P. *Paleobiology of the Invertebrates.* John Wiley & Sons, Inc., 1973.
A very large and rather pretentious book with good illustrations, intended for university students and professional geologists.

WELLER, J. M. *The Course of Evolution.* McGraw-Hill Book Co. Inc., 1969.
An account of the animal and plant kingdoms treated in a rather academic way. Not for most readers of the present book.

WOODS, H. *Paleontology.* Cambridge University Press, 1946.
An old text, revised and reprinted many times. Still useful in some respects but not recommended.

INDEX

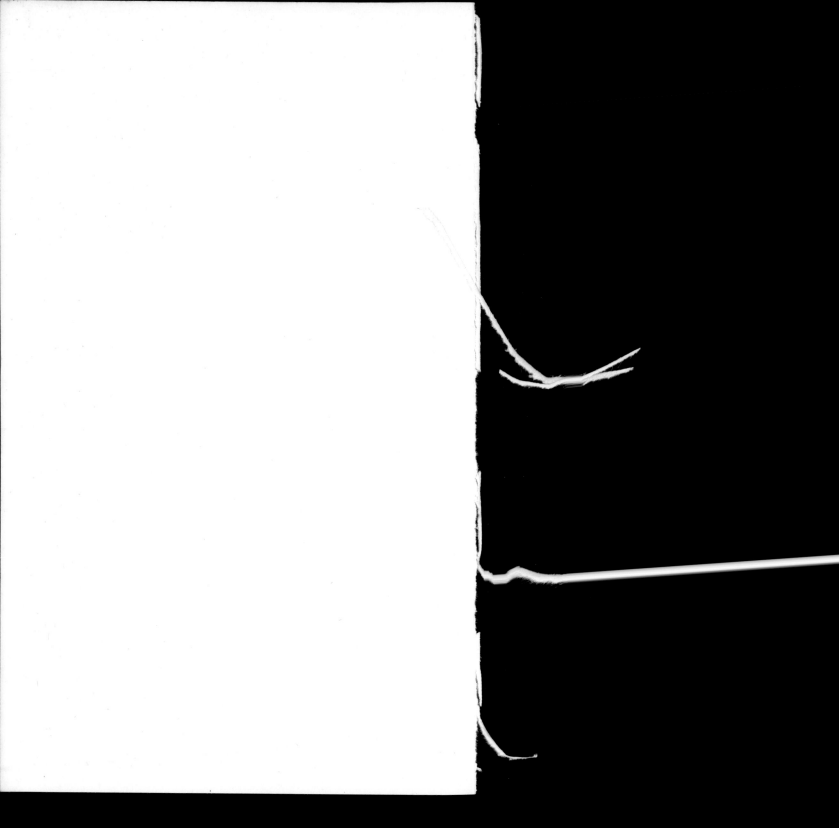